AN ILLUSTRATED GUIDE TO

MODERN

NAVAL

WARFARE

AN ILLUSTRATED GUIDE TO
MODERN
NAVAL
WARFARE

Max Walmer

PRENTICE HALL PRESS
New York   London   Toronto   Sydney   Tokyo

Prentice Hall Press
Gulf + Western Building
One Gulf + Western Plaza
New York, New York 10023

An Arco Military Book

PRENTICE HALL PRESS and colophon are registered trademarks of
Simon & Schuster Inc.

Originally published in 1989 in the United Kingdom by Salamander Books
Ltd., 52 Bedford Row, London WC1R 4LR.

Library of Congress Cataloging-in-Publication Data

Walmer, Max
    Illustrated guide to modern naval warfare/Max Walmer.
        p.   cm. — (An Arco military book)
    ISBN 0-13-451170-0 : $11.95
    1. Naval art and science—History—20th century.   2. Naval
strategy.   3. Naval tactics.   4. Warships.   I. Title.   II. Series.
V53.M55   1989
359'.009'04—dc19   89-3879
                                                                CIP

10 9 8 7 6 5 4 3 2 1

First Prentice Hall Press Edition

Credits

Author: Max Walmer is an experienced writer who has produced many
technical articles and military books, including Salamander's Illustrated
Guides: "Strategic Weapons", "Weapons of the Special Forces" and
"Modern Elite Forces". He has seen extensive service with the British
Armed Forces.

Editor: Graham Smith
Designer: Rod Ferring
Artworks: Maltings Partnership, Tony Gibbons, Terry Hadler, Stephen
Seymour (©Salamander Books Ltd).
Filmset: The Old Mill
Color reproduction by: Magnum Graphics Ltd. and Graham Curtis.
Printed: in Belgium by Proost International Book Production, Turnhout.

Photographs: The publisher wishes to thank all the official government
archives, companies and officials who have supplied pictures for this
book.

Contents

War at Sea

The vastness and complexity of the oceans are too frequently underestimated and it is remarkable that Man knows more about the distant Moon than he does about the oceans which cover 71 per cent of his own planet. The surface of these oceans varies between absolute calm and violent storms with waves of up to 80 to 100ft (25 to 30m) in height and wind speeds of over 100mph (160kmh). Likewise, visibility can change within a few minutes from utter clarity out to the horizon to zero as fog or storms descend. All this creates conditions which are difficult to predict with any accuracy and quite beyond the control of Man — even in this technologically advanced age, the ocean can swallow an 80,000 ton supertanker without trace.

If the two-dimensional surface is neither totally understood nor tamed, the third dimension — the oceanic depths — is even more hostile and unknown. Nearest to land are many shallows, shoals and rocks, which create constant hazards for the unwary mariner. These formations merge and become continental shelves, where the water depth averages less than 425ft (130m), and which extend for up to 40nm (75km) from the land masses. However, this relatively shallow zone accounts for an area of less than 5 per cent of the ocean. To seaward of the continental shelf is the continental slope, a zone where depth increases rapidly from 425ft (130m) to about 6,500ft (2,000m). Beyond this again, the continental rise begins a gradual descent to depths of

Above: HMS *Dreadnought*'s "all-big gun" armament of 10x12in (305mm) guns revolutionised battleship design in 1906.

Below: Pre-Dreadnoughts had a mix of guns. The *Deutschland*, had 4x12in (305mm), 4x10in (254mm) and 12x6in (152mm).

13,000 to 19,500ft (4,000 to 6,000m), where the abyssal plain is characterised by rugged and complex topography with some high peaks and trenches of as much as 36,000ft (11,000m) deep. In this region the ambient temperature can be as low as − 2°C and pressure as great as 2.95 tons/ft² (30 tonnes/m²).

Depth and pressure are not the only characteristics of the oceans. The waters of the world's oceans are continuously on the move, being affected both by daily tidal movements (caused by the gravitational attraction of the moon and sun), and by currents (such as the Gulf Stream) some of which move as fast as 136 miles (250km) per day. Although currents are strongest near the surface of the sea (usually caused by the wind) they occur at all depths, their circulation being three dimensional, with both vertical and horizontal components.

on October 21, 1805, 27 British ships-of-the-line commanded by Admiral Lord Nelson attacked and defeated 33 ships of the combined French and Spanish fleets. The battle lasted just a few hours: it was bitterly contested and the slaughter was great but, as was usual in battles between wooden sailing ships, very few were sunk and the issue was decided in most cases through carrying an opponent by boarding. However, despite his use of new tactics, Nelson's ships and muzzle-loading cannon were technologically little different from those used by Drake in 1588 against the Armada.

The pace of naval technological development started to accelerate in the second half of the nineteenth century with the appearance of steam propulsion, followed by breech-loading guns and, later, by torpedoes and submarines. The climax for

Above: In World War II battleships shared the glory with carriers, but it was their swansong; post-war, the carriers reigned supreme.

Whereas land is characterised by hills and valleys and political boundaries, the surface of the ocean is uniform and there are no frontiers. Thus, by custom developed over the centuries, naval forces can travel at will, moving secretly and appearing from over the horizon to alter the balance of power virtually as and when they wish. Indeed, clashes can even take place at sea which, because the security of neither homeland is directly threatened, need not necessarily escalate into open war.

For the greater part of recorded history warships were propelled by sails, although some used oars (at least during engagements). The greatest sail battle (and the last of any significance) was at Trafalgar, where,

warships, developed during the Victorian era, came at the Battle of Tsushima in May 1905, when the Japanese battle fleet annihilated a Russian fleet which had sailed halfway round the world.

Whereas muzzle-loading cannon had an effective range of some 250 yards (273m), Tsushima was fought at ranges of up to 7,000 yards (6,400m), but under relatively primitive control. With the ever-increasing rate of development, however, ranges opened out further as gun tubes, ammunition and propellants were improved and ranges well in excess of 10 miles (16km) became common. These developments could not, however, be fully exploited until more sophisticated methods of fire control had been incorporated into ships' systems: optical instruments, mechanical computers and centralised control by telephone were needed to control the fire of individual ships while radio was needed to co-ordinate the fire of a fleet to ensure that each ship engaged an appropriate target.

The principle opponents in World War I were the huge British and German fleets, who had several skirmishes but only one great battle: Jutland, May 31, 1916. This battle was on a scale never before envisaged, involving one of the greatest concentrations ever of warships:

Involving five times as many warships as Trafalgar, Jutland was a controversial battle but not as decisive as had been hoped. However, the German fleet, despite having suffered fewer losses than the British, never ventured out to seek battle again.

World War I was the first major

	British		German	
	Strength	Losses	Strength	Losses
Battleships	28		22	1
Battlecruisers	9	3	5	1
Cruisers	33	3	11	4
Seaplane carrier	1			
Minelayer	1			
Destroyers	79	8	72	5
	151	**14**	**110**	**11**

Below: During World War II, US Navy aircraft carriers established themselves as the most powerful single instrument of naval power.

Right: Warships' ability to bombard shore targets has continued to be of value during the Vietnam War (as here) and in the Falklands War.

Below: In World War II, German submarines such as these almost brought Great Britain to the point of starvation in the Battle of the Atlantic.

appearance of the submarine and once the Germans had embarked upon unrestricted use of this new weapon Britain was brought to the verge of starvation. Aircraft, too, joined naval combat and by the end of the war the world's first aircraft carrier was at sea. These novel weapons had to be countered by new weapons and sensors, and the arts of anti-submarine warfare (ASW) and air defence at sea were born, although both were very primitive and ineffective right up to the end of the war.

The first major naval event of the inter-war years was the 1922 Washington Naval Treaty, whose provisions included a pledge not to build any capital ships for ten years and the establishment of a ratio in capital ships of 5:5:3 between Great Britain, the United States and Japan. In 1930 the London Naval Conference confirmed this ratio — much to Japan's fury, which led to her refusing to recognise the Washington Treaty in 1934. This is generally taken as the starting point for the naval arms race.

Developments had, however, been taking place despite treaty restrictions. Aircraft carriers and naval aviation became mature systems, with the Americans, British and Japanese leading the field. The lessons of the war were incorporated into submarine design, while some blind-alleys were also explored (such as steam propulsion, giant "commerce raiders" and aircraft-carrying submarines). Radar and sonar (known as ASDIC in the British Navy) were discovered, making great improvements in ASW and air defence.

World War II involved naval operations on a global scale. The German surface fleet was composed of a relatively small number of warships

of exceptional quality, but they were committed piecemeal and gradually eliminated, although this process tied down the British and (to a lesser extent) the United States navies for some four years. The Italian Navy, too, was slowly whittled away.

It was Allied command of the sea (including the airspace above it) which enabled the great amphibious landings of World War II to take place in North Africa, Sicily, Italy, Southern France and Normandy; it was also Allied naval power which enabled supplies to be transported from the New World to Britain, and from the United States and Britain to Russia.

The great, traditional fleet actions of the war took place in the Pacific, between the Japanese and American fleets, of which Midway (1942) and Leyte Gulf (1944) were arguably the most important. Midway was particularly significant. It was not only the

that passed, making practicable the succession of successful amphibious attacks by which Japan was slowly but surely driven out of the war.

The surface war saw not only the twilight of the strategic influence and tactical power of the battleship, but the emergence of the aircraft carrier as the capital ship. However, some of the greatest and certainly the most protracted naval battles of the war were fought by and against the submarine. In the Atlantic, German submarines repeated the successes of 1916-17 by bringing Britain to the verge of defeat and requiring enormous resources to be devoted to overcoming them. In the Pacific, the powerful Japanese submarine force was surprisingly unsuccessful, failing to repay the investment of resources devoted to building up and maintaining it. American submarines were, however, extremely effective and reduced the Japanese

turning point in which America regained command of the Pacific, but it also signalled the end of the battleship as the supreme weapon afloat — as well as being the first major engagement in which the opposing fleets never came within sight of each other. American dominance of the Pacific increased thereafter with every month

merchant fleet virtually to zero in just three years.

Since World War II the world's navies have developed and been employed at a pace never before equalled in peacetime. Western navies have been used to support land campaigns in Korea, Indochina, Vietnam and Malaya, and to support amphibious operations at Suez and in the Lebanon. There have been numerous naval operations to impose a "presence" and to seek to maintain the freedom of the seas, such as the operations in the Persian Gulf in the mid-1980s. There has also been a constant effort to exert control of the seas by the United States and her allies (particularly through NATO) on the one hand and by the ever-expanding Soviet Navy on the other. Never, however, was the importance of seapower more clearly seen than in the 1982 Falklands War, when the naval task force was absolutely crucial to Britain regaining her lost dependency from Argentina. This conflict also has major significance in that it represents the one realistic test in the post-World War II period of many modern naval tactics, particularly those relating to missiles.

The period has seen the growth of the aircraft carrier into a weapon of enormous strength, with just one American supercarrier carrying an air component more powerful and flexible than the entire air force of many powers. Ironically, the period has,

perhaps, also seen the beginning of the eclipse of the carrier (which now represents an extraordinary concentration of resources making it an exceptionally attractive target) by the submarine.

Despite their successes, World War II submarines were very slow and of limited capability; very few, for example, could dive with any degree of safety to depths greater than their own length. The development of the "snorkel" and streamlined hull forms has greatly increased underwater endurance and speed of diesel-electric submarines, while nuclear propulsion and the use of ever-stronger materials have made possible protracted operations at great depths and speeds. Finally, underwater-launched ballistic and cruise missiles have given submarines capabilities against land targets and ships, which make them the capital ships of today. So great, indeed, is the submarine threat that the major effort in most of today's navies (apart from operating sub marines) is now devoted to anti-submarine warfare and its associated technologies.

Left: These Sea Harriers aboard HMS *Hermes* during the 1982 Falklands War were the first naval V/STOL aircraft to be committed to combat. Four navies already operate them and Italy may soon join their number.

Below: Modern surface warships, such as this US Navy Spruance class destroyer, *John Young* (DD973) are highly complex, very powerful and extremely expensive, both to build and to maintain.

Naval Forces

At the end of World War II the naval scene seemed fairly straightforward. The day of the battleship and battlecruiser was clearly over, their role having been assumed by the aircraft carrier. The US Navy had a sizeable carrier fleet and were clearly determined to stay in the business, building ever larger carriers. The British had a smaller number of carriers and a few other navies had one or at most two carriers each. There was a large number of cruisers, whose post-war role was a little unclear, and vast numbers of destroyers, frigates and corvettes whose role in escorting carriers and in combatting the ever-growing threat of the submarine was crystal clear.

The two great navies were those of the United States and Great Britain, two nations whose global responsibilities could only be met by deploying large fleets. The German and

Japanese fleets had been totally destroyed or taken over as war booty. The Soviet Navy was relatively small, had played a limited role during the war and seemed to be content to confine itself to the coastal waters of the USSR. The remaining fleets of other nations were small and of little global strategic consequence, except where they belonged to a larger alliance.

There had been violent and far-ranging submarine campaigns in the Atlantic and Pacific Oceans, with vast tonnages of surface shipping sunk, as well as many submarines. The great majority of submarine fleets were composed of boats little improved from those at sea in 1939, and which were essentially slow-moving, limited-endurance submersibles. Just as the war was ending, however, the German Type XXI appeared, which used streamlining and greater power to attain much higher submerged speeds. Even so, these fine boats were still compelled to approach within snorkel distance of the surface regularly in order to run their diesel engines and recharge the batteries.

Above: The very epitome of battleship might, USS *Missouri* (BB63) and *New Jersey* (BB62) lie in Yokosuka Harbor, Japan in 1953. The battleship was then considered a dying breed and few would have dared forecast that both ships would still be in frontline service 35 years later.

Left: In the early 1920s USS *Saratoga* (CV3) (seen here), together with her sister *Lexington* (CV2), was converted while building from a battlecruiser to an aircraft carrier. Their aircraft complement was 18 fighters, 40 bombers and 5 utility machines.

Aircraft Carriers

In the early post-war years the American and British navies devoted much energy to adjusting to the advent of turbojet aircraft. Development work was concentrated on the aircraft themselves and their engines, but the ships, too, needed change. There were three crucial inventions: the steam catapult, the deck-landing mirror, and the angled flight-deck. At the same time the US Navy was determined to have its own nuclear role and produced bombers such as the North American AJ-2 Savage and the Douglas A-3 Skywarrior. Even larger carriers were needed to carry such bombers, and a number of classes were constructed, name ships of which were the *Forrestal* (78,000 tons), the nuclear-powered *Enterprise* (89,600 tons) and *Nimitz* (91,400 tons), together with the non-nuclear *Kitty Hawk* (82,000 tons). The US Navy today has a fleet of 15 aircraft carriers,

with a further three nuclear-powered ships under construction.

The Royal Navy's carrier force peaked in operational capability and excellence in the mid-1960s with some good carriers (*Ark Royal, Eagle, Victorious* and *Hermes*) and capable air wings. A crisis developed, however, when the needs for a new carrier (CVA 01), new escorts (the Type 82 destroyer) and new aircraft all coincided, and the British defence budget proved incapable of accommodating them. Much work had been done on a new carrier design, but it was cancelled. After such a debacle it appeared for a while as if the Fleet Air Arm would be confined to helicopters, but authority was obtained to build three ships which were originally described as "through-deck cruisers", but which are now properly designated as light aircraft carriers — the *Illustrious* (19,812 tons), operating the V/STOL Sea Harrier, is the name ship of the class.

Below: Soviet carrier *Novorossiysk* combines V/STOL aircraft and helicopters with a very heavy and effective missile armament.

The French Navy spent the first few post-war years with just one ex-British aircraft carrier, but they then built two or their own design in the late-1950s. These ships, *Clemenceau* and *Foch* (32,780 tons), have served the French well and will be replaced in the 1990s by two nuclear-powered aircraft carriers of the de Gaulle class (PAN 1).

Above: US Navy Forrestal class carrier *Saratoga* (CV60).

Above: British *Ark Royal* with Sea Harriers and "ski-jump".

It is in the USSR, however, that some of the most interesting developments have taken place, starting with the *Moskva* (18,000 tons), a helicopter-carrying ASW cruiser, and followed by the *Kiev* (38,000 tons), name ship of a new class of carrier. The Soviet Navy is working to a long-range plan to develop a fully capable air arm of its own, and, as this is a completely new field for them, they are unfettered by traditional practices and out-of-date ideas. Thus, *Kiev* introduced many novel ideas and it seems that the new nuclear-powered Kremlin class carriers will continue that process.

Smaller navies traditionally purchased surplus aircraft carriers from either the American or British navies, and the navies of India, Argentina and Brazil are still so equipped. Such sources have, however, now dried-up. The Spanish and Italian navies have recently produced their own, first-ever, light aircraft carriers, based on the use of helicopters and V/STOL aircraft. These designs are very attractive to navies seeking to enter the aircraft carrier "club" or needing to replace existing carriers.

Battleships and Battlecruisers

In the immediate post-war years older battleships and battlecruisers were rapidly scrapped, although the Korean War revived the need for shore bombardment and all four US Navy Iowa class battleships saw service there before being "mothballed" in 1954-58. By 1960 the only battleships left were these four Iowas, the British *Vanguard*, and the French *Jean Bart* and *Richelieu*. The British and the French, however, consigned these last remaining capital ships to the scrapyards and the Iowas were left in reserve, regarded by many as simply objects of curiosity. The shore bombardment role reappeared during the Vietnam War and one of the Iowas, the *New Jersey*, was reactivated during the years 1967 to 1969 before being put back into reserve once more. The battleship story might well have ended there had it not been for the appearance of the Soviet Kirov class in the late-1970s.

From the mid-1960s onwards the Soviets, rather than follow patterns established by other countries, started producing original concepts of their own. One startling example was the *Kirov*, which appeared in 1977, by far the largest surface warship (aircraft carriers excepted) to be built since 1945. Of 28,000 tons displacement, fast, long-ranged, with no discernible armoured protection and with a heavy anti-ship missile armament, the *Kirov* is in many ways a totally new concept, but there is, nevertheless, a strong relationship with the battlecruisers of a previous era.

Faced with this new Soviet threat the US Navy decided to refurbish the four Iowa class battleships, which were still in excellent condition. Described as a "valuable supplement to the carrier force" all four have now returned to service. A plan to replace the after 16in (406mm) turret with a large flight-deck was shelved on cost grounds in favour of a less drastic and much cheaper solution, but with nine 16in (406mm) guns, and 32 Tomahawk and 16 Harpoon missiles, coupled with high speed and excellent armoured protection these are very formidable ships. Indeed, their armour makes them relatively immune to anti-ship missiles. It seems very doubtful that any new battleships of the size and complexity of the Iowas will be built, but then nobody had expected the Soviet Navy to build the *Kirov*.

Below Left: USS *New Jersey* (BB62) combines the power of 16in (406mm) and 5in (127mm) guns with contemporary missiles, such as Tomahawk (32) and Harpoon (16).

Below Centre: Return of the US battleships was spurred by the appearance of this Soviet Kirov class battlecruiser, largest warship (apart from carriers) built since World War II.

Below: USS *New Jersey* and her three sisters combine firepower with protection unmatched even by the Soviet Kirovs. The main 12in (305mm) armoured belt is impervious to anti-ship missiles, which are designed to attack thin-skinned warships.

Cruisers

The masses of war-built cruisers sufficed most navies well into the 1960s, except for the USSR. Starting with the *Sverdlov* (17,200 tons) the Soviets built 14 of this class, the last all-gun cruisers to be built. The Sverdlovs were followed by: in the 1960s, the Kynda class (5,550 tons), which combined a gun armament with eight SS-N-3 anti-ship missiles; in the 1970s, the Kresta class (7,600 tons) and the Kara class (9,700 tons); and, in the 1980s, by the Slava class (12,500 tons). Each class has been larger than the last, carrying the latest guns and missiles, together with an ever-increasing variety of sensors. There are currently 39 cruisers serving with the Soviet Navy, of which eleven are the survivors of the Sverdlov class.

There was little new construction in the United States until the late-1950s when USS *Long Beach* (17,525 tons) was built. This was the world's first nuclear-powered surface warship and the first to have a guided-missile main battery. Since then there has been a steady stream of nuclear-powered, guided-missile cruisers: *Bainbridge* (8,592 tons) commissioned in 1962, *Truxtun* (9,127 tons) (1967), two California class (9,561 tons) (1974-75), and four Virginia class (10,000 tons) (1976-80). The US Navy has also produced a series of non-nuclear powered cruisers of the *Leahy* (5,670 tons) (1962-64) and *Belknap* (8,200 tons) (1964-67) classes.

By the early-1970s the benefits of propulsion by nuclear-power — primarily long range and the reduction in fleet trains — were starting to be offset by the enormous capital costs, and when faced with a bid by the US Navy for a numerically large class of cruisers to take the Aegis air defence system Congress insisted that the oil-fired Spruance design be used as the starting point for the new class of Aegis cruisers and not the nuclear-powered Virginia. The result was the *Ticonderoga* (9,000 tons) guided-missile cruiser.

This class (CG 47) is a series of effective ships with outstanding air defence and air direction capabilities; at least 27 will be built, making it one of the most significant of contemporary warship designs. Intended for the anti-air mission, but with some surface and ASW capability, these cruisers act as screens for carrier task groups.

The US Navy currently possesses 9 nuclear-powered and 27 conventionally-powered cruisers, with another 18 of the Ticonderoga class due to join the fleet over the next few years. Today the Royal Navy officially has no cruisers at all, although *HMS Bristol* (7,100 tons), the sole Type 82 destroyer, is every bit as large as the class which includes the Soviet *Kynda* and the American *Leahy* cruisers. France has one modern cruiser and Italy two, while Peru and Chile each have two elderly World War II vintage cruisers.

There is little international consensus on a uniform system of designation for warships in the 2,000 to 8,000 tons bracket. The Royal Navy designates the Type 42 class (4,100 tons) as destroyers but the larger type 22s (4,900 tons) are frigates. NATO classifies the Soviet Kynda class (5,560 tons) as cruisers, but the 8,000 ton Udaloys as destroyers. In the United States, escort ships of 10,000 tons (Virginia class), classified in the 1970s as "frigates", are now designated "cruisers". The Spruance class (7,810 tons) warships are classified as destroyers while the Ticonderoga class, on an identical hull but with a greater displacement (9,600 tons) are cruisers.

Compounding confusion the French Navy originally rated the Type C67 class (5,745 tons) as corvettes, but then re-rated them as frigates, although giving them "D" (destroyer) rather than "F" (frigate) pennant numbers, which would have been logical! Nor have the French dropped the designation "corvette", however, as they have rated their newest class, the C70 (4,170 tons), as corvettes, although these, too, have "D" pennant numbers! Rather than try to devise a new and more logical system, this book uses the ship designations as given by the respective navies, or by NATO in the case of Warsaw Pact warships.

Above: The Soviet Navy has some impressive cruisers, such as this Kara class, 9,700 tons.

Below: USS *Ticonderoga* (C47), 9,589 tons, nameship of a class of 27 building for the US Navy.

Below: The nuclear-powered cruiser USS *Virginia* (CGN38), 11,300 tons, is designed to operate for ten years on one fuelling.

Destroyers and Frigates

The problem facing virtually all navies is that the price of warships has soared and for the great majority of navies a hull of about 4,000 tons is as large as they can afford, in terms of finance, manpower, construction and dockyard facilities. These medium-sized ships are required to fulfil a number of roles which require them to be able to deal with threats from the air, from surface-skimming missiles, from other surface warships and from submarines; in other words a "maid-of-all-work" in most fleets.

The backbone of the US escort fleet is the Spruance class of 31 ships, optimised for the ASW mission. The four-ship Kidd class must be included as they are very similar, having been ordered by the Shah of Iran.

The Shah was deposed before they could be delivered and they were eventually bought for the US Navy, making a very useful addition to the fleet. The remaining US destroyers are ten Coontz class and 23 Charles F Adams class, most of which are due to be given a "DDG mid-life upgrade", but the Navy's plans now centre upon the Arleigh Burke (DDG 51) class, 29 of which are planned, to be followed by 31 of an "Improved Arleigh Burke" design.

The US Navy has a large frigate fleet, numbering 116, the oldest of which, the Bronstein class (2,690 tons), date back to 1963. The majority, however, are the 51 (plus one still building) of the Oliver Hazard Perry (FFG 7) class, large vessels of 3,585 tons displacement, which makes them equal in size to "destroyers" in many other navies.

The Soviet Navy built many destroyers as part of the great post-war naval expansion plan; 44 of these Skory, Kotlin, SAM Kotlin, Kanin and Kildin classes remain in service, with more in reserve. After these (1963 to 1972) came the Kashin class (4,500 tons), the first major warships in the world to be powered exclusively by gas-turbines; 13 are still in service, plus six of the "Modified Kashin" class. There then followed a lengthy gap before the Sovremenny class (7,900 tons) and Udaloy class (8,000 tons) were laid down in 1976 and 1978 respectively.

The Sovremenny class is optimised for the surface and anti-air role with a heavy missile and gun armament, together with a Kamov Ka-32 Helix Helicopter. The Udaloy class is optimised for the ASW role and uses a totally different hull design from that of the Sovremenny. Six Sovremenny and eight Udaloy destroyers are in service, with at least two more of each class building.

The Soviet Navy also has a large number of frigates, of which the major units are the Krivak class, 33 strong, with one more building. Virtually all Western frigates are designed as convoy (and especially merchant convoy) escorts, but this is a role which is not

Below: HMS *Edinburgh*, one of four British Type 42 Batch 3 destroyers, incorporates the lessons learned at such cost in the Falklands War.

really required in the Soviet Navy and most frigates, particularly the Krivak class, are therefore designed as escorts for task groups.

The latest Royal Navy destroyer class is the Type 42 (4,100 tons). Designed for area air defence of a task group, these ships have a mixed gun and missile armament; the latest to be constructed (Batch 3) have been stretched by some 51ft (16m) in overall length to accommodate better weapons systems and to improve speed and speakeeping.

For some years the Royal Navy frigate fleet has centred upon the very successful Leander class (2,700 tons), which have helicopter facilities, VDS and long-range radar.

The successor to the Leander class is the Type 22 (4,200 tons, Batch 1; 4,900 tons, Batch 3) which, like the Type 42 destroyers, has been stretched and considerably altered in appearance; 14 are being built. This class will be succeeded by the Type 23 frigate, the first of which has recently been ordered. There has been considerable controversy over this design,

the arguments centring upon the efforts to reconcile the lessons of the Falklands War with the problem of keeping expenditure within the limits set by a restricted national defence budget. Current Royal Navy front-line strength in these two classes is 13 destroyers and 44 frigates with four building.

The Japanese Maritime Self-Defence Force (JMSDF) has built an interesting destroyer and frigate fleet, with a clear policy of constant improvement in a succession of inter-related classes. In the destroyer class they are following two separate, mission-oriented lines of development — one for air defence/surface warfare and the second for ASW. Their destroyers tend to be large, handsome, well armed and with a very comprehensive electronic equipment fit, as would be expected from a nation with such a strong electronics industry. There are 34 destroyers in service, the main current designs being the Hatsayuki (3,800 tons) class and the latest air defence type, the Hatakaze (4,600 tons) class.

Below: USS *Radford* (DD968), one of the very successful, 31-strong Spruance class, the US Navy's largest post-war destroyer programme.

France has a great tradition of imaginative and effective destroyer design, and, like the Japanese, has followed a policy of gradual improvement over a number of small classes. The French are also now producing separate anti-air and ASW designs, the latest being the Georges Leygues (ASW) class and Cassard (AA) class, which are good examples of the recent trend to use the same hull for two different roles and weapon/sensor fits. The total number of destroyers in service is 19. French frigates *(avisos)* are a little different in concept to those in other navies, as they are built with a colonial policing role very much in mind. The resulting ships are rather small, but very well armed and with long ranges. There are 25 in service, with more building.

The Italian Navy, like that of the French, has a long history of large, effective destroyer designs, and has produced a series of classes since the war. They currently have four destroyers in service of which the latest class, the two-strong Audace class (4,400 tons) is very impressive. There are 16 frigates in service, of four classes, the latest of which, the *Maestrale* (3,040 tons), is well armed and equipped, and, like all Italian ships, exceptionally fast.

The other navy with a significant fleet in this area is that of the Netherlands, who have produced a series of exceptional designs in their own yards in order to be able to operate three balanced task groups as part of NATO's EASTLANT command. Initially, the Dutch built six British-designed Leander class (2,835 tons) frigates (van Speijk class), and followed them with two large and very powerful frigates of their own design, the Tromp class (4,308 tons), which are equivalent in every way to the "destroyers" of other navies. An attempt at agreeing a collaborative venture with the British having failed, the Dutch then produced the Kortenaer class (3,630 tons); they have built ten ships for themselves and two for Greece, while a further six

have been produced to a slightly modified design in West Germany as the Bremen class (3,600 tons). Two anti-aircraft frigates of the Jakob van Heemskerck class (3,750 tons) are also under construction. A further four frigates of the new "M" class (3,050 tons) are on order, the first of which joined the fleet in 1988.

The Royal Canadian Navy built a series of very adventurous and unusual frigate designs in the 1950s and 1960s (of which 19 are still in service), and an equally unusual destroyer, the DD 280 class (4,700 tons) (four ships) in the early-1970s. There was then a complete gap in shipbuilding, primarily due to budgeting problems, and many of these ships are now very elderly. At last, however, a new class — the Halifax class (4,254 tons) — of six destroyers has been announced, which are due to be commissioned between 1989 and 1992.

Large numbers of destroyers and frigates serve with smaller navies, most of them being export versions of other nation's designs, mainly originating from the United States, the USSR, Britain, France, Italy, Federal Germany, Spain and China.

Right: *Udaloy*, name ship of the latest Soviet Navy destroyer class. Displacing 7,900 tons, they would be classified as cruisers in Western navies.

Above: The two Tromp class destroyers are task group flagships in the small, but highly efficient Dutch Navy.

Below: The French destroyer *Suffren* launching a Masurca SAM. This missile has a range of over 30nm.

Corvettes

Corvettes went out of fashion after the end of World War II. There has been a revival in the past decade, and some smaller navies have opted for corvettes of between 500 and 1,000 tons displacement, an intermediate type between frigates and fast attack craft. The Finnish Turunmaa class manages to mount a 4.7in (120mm) gun, plus two 40mm and two 20mm cannon, as well as depth-charge racks and anti-submarine rockets on a 770 ton hull. Vosper Thornycroft have sold a number of their corvette designs to various navies, including the Mark 9, which mounts a 76mm gun, one 40mm and two 20mm cannon, an ASW rocket launcher and a Seacat SAM launcher on a 780 ton hull.

The Soviet Navy has produced a series of capable light combatants. The Nanuchka III class (660 tons), is armed with six SS-N-9 SSMs, two twin SA-N-4 launchers, one 76mm gun and one 30mm Gatling CIWS. The slightly smaller Tarantul II class (587 tons) mounts four SS-N-22, one quad SA-N-5, one 76mm gun and two 30mm Gatling CIWS. Both of these classes are capable of a top speed of 36 knots. The Pauk class uses the Tarantul hull, but is optimised for the ASW role and is powered by diesels rather than gas turbines. It is armed with SA-N-5, one 76mm gun and one 30mm gatling CIWS, together with the ASW armament of four torpedo tubes, two RBU-1200 rocket launchers, and two depth-charge racks.

These small warships, although heavily armed, are not the complete answer to a navy's problems of size and cost. Nothing is ever obtained without penalty; in the case of corvettes and fast attack craft, the heavy weapons and sensor fit is only feasible at the expense of speed, range and seakeeping qualities.

Below: Egyptian Osa class was supplied by the USSR, one of many such missile-armed fast patrol boats in service around the world.

Right: Sparviero class hydrofoil of the Italian Navy is armed with two Otomat SSMs and a 76mm Compact gun. Top speed in calm sea is 50 knots.

Fast Attack Craft

Fast attack craft (FAC) are the successors to World War II motor torpedo boats (MTBs), motor gun boats (MGBs) and patrol torpedo (PT) boats. Several hundred FACs are in service with many navies, some with conventional hulls and others with hydrofoils. Fast attack craft achieved international prominence when an Egyptian Osa class FAC sank the Israel destroyer *Eilat*, demonstrating that missiles give these craft a previously inconceivable hitting power. Among current boats, for example, the Israeli Romat class (488 tons) mounts six Gabriel and eight Harpoon SSMs, while the West German Type 148 (265 tons) has four Exocet and one 76mm gun.

Amphibious Warfare Ships

For many years after World War II the only navies to retain a significant amphibious capability were those of the United States and Great Britain, with the French some way behind. Thus, the US Navy was able to mount a major amphibious landing at Inchon in 1952, and the British and French navies a similar operation at Suez in 1956. Thereafter, there were only some very minor landings until the British operation to retake the Falkland Islands in 1982, when virtually her entire remaining amphibious warfare fleet was mobilised.

The major developments in amphibious warfare have been the introduction of helicopters, air-cushion vehicles (ACV) and the V/STOL aircraft, all of which have contributed to easing the problem of getting over the first, critical and most vulnerable stage of a landing operation.

The US Navy has developed a series of large assault ships, first the Iwo Jima class (18,825 tons) (seven in service) and then the very large and capable Tarawa class (39,300 tons) (five in service). The Tarawa class can embark a Marine Corps battalion landing-team of some 1,900 men plus various mixes of CH-53 Sea Stallion, CH-46 Sea Knight helicopters and AV-8A/B Harriers, together with four large and six small landing-craft.

The Soviet Navy has developed a global amphibious warfare capability, which, although not yet challenging the US Navy in numbers or capability, is nevertheless strong and growing every year. The Soviet amphibious fleet currently comprises 17 Ropucha class LSTs (3,800 tons), 14 Alligator class LSTs (4,700 tons) and 43 Polnochny class LSMs (800 tons). Most impressive are the two Ivan Rogov class LPDs (13,000 tons), each of which carries a battalion group of Soviet Naval Infantry together with two ACVs, a number of landing-craft and some helicopters.

Most other navies have a limited amphibious capability, usually consisting of a small number of LPDs, LSTs and LCTs. Only the United States and the USSR have an ACV capability, with the Soviet Navy currently far ahead of the US Navy in this respect. The Soviet Pomornik class (360 tons) ACV can carry up to four PT-76 light tanks or some 220 troops at speeds of up to 55 knots. They are driven by five gas turbines, three driving ducted propellers and two the lift fans. The vessels are armed with two SA-N-5/8 SAM launchers and two 30mm Gatling CIWS. There have also been persistent rumours of a Wing-in-Ground Effect (WIG) craft being developed for both assault landing and anti-ship roles. Despite numerous "artist's impressions" no firm proof of the WIG's existence has been forthcoming.

Below: USS *Guadalcanal*, one of seven Iwo Jima class helicopter carriers. They usually carry a mix of CH-53 and CH-46 transport and AH-1 attack helicopters, but can also embark RH-53/MH-53E minesweeping helicopters or AV-8B V/STOL Harriers.

Above: *Ivan Rogov* is one of two
very large landing ships in the
expanding Soviet amphibious
warfare fleet. She is fitted with
bow and stern doors, and the
helicopter hangar serves two
landing spots, one on the
foredeck and the other over the
stern. Three Lebed class ACVs
can use the docking well.

Right: US Marine Corps LVTP-7
amphibious APC leaves the ramp
of a US Navy landing ship. The
ability to deploy such forces
confers a major strategic
advantage on the United States,
a lesson which the Soviets learnt
in the 1950s and 1960s, leading
to the expansion of their
amphibious warfare capability in
the past 20 years.

Submarines

There were several occasions in World War II when German U-boats brought Britain to the brink of starvation. At the same time the US Navy's submarines in the Pacific were winning a great victory against the Japanese, whose merchant fleet was reduced to a critical level. This mission of attacking hostile naval surface warships and maritime logistic traffic remained the submarine's primary strategic role until the mid-1960s. Then the development of submarine-launched ballistic missiles (SLBM) and submarine-launched cruise missiles (SLCM) added a further and even more important strategic role — that of striking directly at targets in the enemy's homeland.

Only the six most advanced navies (China, France, Great Britain, India, the USSR and the United States) currently operate nuclear-powered submarines, although Argentina, Brazil, Canada and Spain are giving serious consideration to nuclear-propulsion for their next generation of attack submarines. Of the navies currently operating nuclear submarines, only the US Navy and French Navy intend to go "all-nuclear". Other navies will retain diesel-electric boats.

The Soviet Navy operates the world's largest submarine fleet. Its five Typhoon class (25,000 tons) SSBNs are the largest submarines ever built — by a very large margin. They are armed with 20 SS-N-20 SLBMs. There are also four Delta IV, 14 Delta III, four Delta II and 18 Delta I. Of the older Yankee class, 17 remain in service as SSBNs, but some have now been converted to either SSN or SSGN roles. One elderly Hotel class SSBN and one Golf class SSB remain in service, but are almost certainly employed in a training or trials role, and are not operational.

The Soviet SSGN/SSG fleet is also large. There are four Oscar class (16,000 tons), 15 Charlie class and 26 Echo class, together with 14 diesel-electric Juliett class SSGs.

There are, too, 79 SSNs in service of eight classes, with no less than three SSN under construction simultaneously, an indication of the enormous scope of the Soviet defence programme. Finally, the Soviet Navy has the world's largest fleet of diesel-electric submarines, with some 135 in service, many quite elderly, but the Tango class (3,900 tons) and the latest Kilo class (3,200 tons) are both ultra-modern and very capable.

The United States submarine fleet is less numerous than that of the USSR, but is very powerful and capable. The latest Ohio class (18,750 tons) SSBNs carry 24 Trident SLBMs, the largest payload of any SSBN; eight are in service, with a further 12 to follow. There are also 28 Lafayette class (8,250 tons), of which 12 have been converted to take the Trident-I (C-4) missile, while the remainder still carry the older Poseidon (C-3) missile.

Right: USS *Ohio*, name ship of a class of at least 20 boats built to carry Trident missiles.

Below: British Resolution class SSBN carries 16 Polaris SLBMs, with British Chevaline warheads.

Mainstay of the SSN fleet is the Los Angeles class (6,900 tons); 37 are in service, with another 29 on order. There are also 37 Sturgeon class (4,640 tons), 13 Permit class (4,470 tons) and three elderly Skipjack class (3,500 tons) boats. Two "one-off" boats, the *Lipscomb* (6,480 tons) and the *Narwhal* (5,830 tons), built to test different propulsion systems, are fully operational. The last remaining operational diesel-electric boats are three Barbel class (2,894 tons) units and the *Darter* (2,250 tons). Finally, two former SSBNs have had their missile-related equipment removed and are now classed as SSNs, but their role is as covert transports, carrying 67 SEAL swimmers and a swimmer delivery vehicle.

Great Britain has four Resolution class (8,500 tons) SSBNs with Polaris A-3TK missiles, which will be replaced in the 1990s by four new Vanguard class (15,850 tons) boats armed with 16 Trident-II (D-5) SLBMs. There are 16 SSNs in service of three classes, the latest being the Trafalgar class (5,280 tons), with four in service and three more building. HMS *Conqueror* holds the distinction of being the only SSN in any navy to have sunk a hostile warship (ARE *General Belgrano*). The Royal Navy still uses conventional submarines, with 12 currently in service: 11 of the elderly Oberon class (2,450 tons) and the first of the new Upholder class (2,400 tons) (at least eight are expected to be ordered).

France has six SSBNs in service and three Rubis class (2,670 tons) SSNs, having decided, for political reasons, to build SSBNs first rather than SSNs, as had been done by the United States, the USSR and Britain. The rest of the fleet comprises four Agosta class (1,740 tons) and nine

Below: Soviet Victor I class nuclear-propelled attack submarine. The first really successful SSNs, 16 Victor Is entered service between 1968 and 1975, and now form part of the 80-strong Soviet SSN fleet. The latest types are much quieter than these Victors and much more difficult for Western ASW sensors to detect.

Right: The first-ever nuclear-powered submarine, USS *Nautilus*, entered service in 1955. However, it was not until 27 years later that this British submarine, HMS *Conqueror*, became the first SSN to sink a hostile ship when she sank the Argentine cruiser ARA *General Belgrano* during the 1982 Falklands War.

Daphne class (1,043 tons), all diesel-electric boats.

The People's Republic of China has three Xia class (7,000 tons) SSBNs and three Han class (4,500 tons) SSNs, all of indigenous design and about which little is known. She also has over 100 diesel-electric boats; the three Ming class (2,113 tons) SSKs are of Chinese design and construction, while the remainder are Soviet Romeo and Whiskey designs, but built in China.

Of the remaining navies many have a small number of submarines, mostly of American, Soviet, French, German or British design. The most significant of these is the Indian Navy, which currently has two Soviet Kilo SSKs (2,900 tons) (with three more on order), two West German Type 1500 SSKs (1,860 tons) (with four more building in Indian yards), and one Soviet Charlie I SSGN on loan, probably the precursor of a new class of SSNs.

Weapons and Armament

The weapons a warship employs are a manifestation of national design philosophies, although initial impressions may sometimes be misleading. For example, a study of contemporary surface warships indicates that Soviet Navy operational requirements give top priority to weapons systems, followed by propulsion, electronics, endurance and, finally, habitability. On the other hand, most Western naval staffs appear to give top priority to electronics and then to habitability, weapons systems, propulsion and, finally, endurance.

Soviet naval weapons, however, tend to be very obvious; the Slava class cruisers bristle with weaponry, their most striking feature being eight twin SS-N-12 ASM launchers lined up either side of the bridge, with a twin 130mm gun turret in the bows. AD armament comprises eight SA-N-6 and two SA-N-4 launchers, together with six 30mm Gatlings, while ASW systems include two quintuple torpedo tubes, two RBU-6000 rocket launchers and a Hormone-B helicopter.

The nearest United States equivalent is the USS *Virginia*, whose surface weaponry includes two 5in (127mm) Mark 45 single gun turrets and two quad Harpoon launchers, with an AD armament of two twin Mark 26 launchers (for Standard SM-2MR missiles) and two Phalanx Mark 26 20mm CIWS. ASW fit includes ASROC (fired from the same launchers as the Standard AAMs) and two triple Mark 32 torpedo tubes.

Every bit of deck-space on the *Slava* is taken up with something, while the *Virginia* has large areas of totally free deck. But, despite the apparent disparity in weaponry, *Virginia* is as well armed as *Slava* and certainly has more reloads, perhaps reflecting the different concepts of a future conflict: the Soviets aiming for an all-out, short-lived onslaught, whereas the United States expects a more protracted campaign.

Below: US Navy's new Arleigh Burke class destroyers will have clear decks with no less than 98 missiles hidden in vertical launchers. They will also incorporate 130 tons of armour to protect vital areas.

Guns

Advocates of missile armament were powerful in many navies in the 1960s and 1970s, and they proposed doing away with guns altogether. Indeed, some warships actually appeared with only a token gun armament; for example, the British Type 22 had just two 40mm guns. The folly of this has been recognised and the need for at least one effective gun now seems to be agreed by every navy.

16in (406mm) guns

By far the largest gun currently in service is the US Navy's 16in (406mm), of which nine are mounted in three 3-gun Mark 7 mounts on each of the Iowa class battleships. (They are "3-gun" rather than "triple" turrets, since each gun is mounted in an individual slide and can be elevated independently of the other two; a triple turret has one slide with all guns being elevated by one drive.)

These guns fire several types of projectile. The Mark 8 AP round weighs 2,700lb (1,225kg); muzzle velocity is 2,425ft/sec, maximum range is 40,185 yards (36,745m). The Mark 13 HC round weighs 1,900lb (862kg), of which 154lb (70kg) is the HE payload; maximum range is 41,600 yards (38,040m). There are also four modern special purpose rounds using the Mark 13 body:

— Mark 143 HE is Mark 13 with M732 proximity fuse.
— Mark 144 improved conventional munition (ICM) dispenses 400 wedge grenades, using the M724 electronic time fuse (ETF).
— Mark 145 HE dispenses 666 shaped-charge "bomblets", using M724 ETF.
— Mark 146 ICM also dispenses 666 "bomblets", using M724 ETF.

A 16in (406mm) nuclear round was tested in the 1950s and seems to have been produced in limited numbers, but was retired in 1961. A new discarding-sabot, extended-range, HE round is under development; with a 13in (33cm) body it is designed to have a range greater than 70,000 yards (64,000m).

These are weapons of awesome power and there is no warship at sea today capable of withstanding them. Their weight, volume requirements and great cost make it highly unlikely that guns of this calibre will ever be made again, and even the latest *Kirov* class battlecruisers only mount one twin 5.1in (130mm) turret.

Below: An Iowa class battleship lets rip with a broadside from her 16in (406mm) guns. The recoil forces and blast overpressure from these guns demand extensive strengthening of the decks and hull.

Dual-purpose guns

Weapons designers have been particularly successful in reducing weight and increasing automation. The US Navy's 5in (127mm) Mark 45 weighs 24.6 tons (25,000kg) and fires 20 rounds per minute; total crew is six, none of whom are in the turret. Another successful Western gun is the OTO Melara single 3in (76.3mm) which has a firing rate variable between 10 and 85rpm. In service with 35 navies, the total installation weight is 7.38 tons (7,500kg). The Soviet Navy has a successful 76.2mm DP twin mount, with a rate of fire of 45rpm/barrel and a maximum effective range in the AA role of 23,000ft (7,000m).

Close-in weapons systems (CIWS)

The threat from air attack and sea-skimming missiles has given rise to a requirement for gun/cannon-based close-in weapons systems (CIWS) for "last-ditch" defence, in which fast reaction times, extremely rapid tracking and a heavy volume of fire are absolutely essential. The US Navy's answer is the Mark 15 Vulcan/Phalanx 20mm, which marries the M61A1 multi-barrel Gatling gun to a very intelligent control system, in which the radar tracks the outgoing projectile and the incoming missile, and seeks to eliminate the difference. The Mark 15 CIWS is completely self-contained and has proved highly successful in service; it was bought as a matter of operational urgency by the Royal Navy for installation in the Illustrious class aircraft carriers, following the 1982 Falklands War.

Other "stand-alone" CIWS include the seven-barrelled Goalkeeper, by Hollandse Signaal Apparat (HSA), which has a rate of fire of some 4,200 rounds per minute. Using the same gun and ammunition as the USAF A-10 tankbuster, this system is being installed in the Dutch Kortenaer class frigates and has also been ordered by the Royal Navy as its standard CIWS. The 30mm CIWS on Soviet ships, a 6-barrelled Gatling design, utilises the separately mounted Bass Tilt radar. Nevertheless, it is an extremely neat installation and is fitted to at least 20 classes of Soviet warship.

A variation on this theme is the Spanish Meroka, which consists of two rows of six 20mm Oerlikon guns, mounted in a conventional turret. Maximum rate of fire for the mount is 9,000rpm and the system incorporates a Lockheed Electronics Sharpshooter x-band monopulse radar on the mount, with a separate search radar.

Above: Guns are highly effective. Amongst the best in service is the OTO Melara 127mm, seen here on the Italian destroyer *Audace*.

Above: The missile threat is being countered by close-in weapons systems (CIWS) such as this US 20mm Mark 15 Vulcan/Phalanx.

Light guns

Apart from these purpose-built CIWS there is a host of small calibre guns and cannon in service for use against surface and air targets at shorter ranges. The venerable, but still effective 20mm Oerlikon is still widely used and the Royal Navy purchased large numbers of GAM-B01 mounts in 1982-83 for numerous vessels as a result of the air threat revealed during the Falklands War. The equally old 40mm Bofors L70 is also widely used, the latest version having a firing rate of 320rpm and a range of 4,374 yards (4,000m).

Below: The Greek frigate *Limnos* uses the highly successful OTO Melara 76.2mm dual purpose remote controlled gun.

Torpedoes

Torpedoes have been the subject of some very expensive (and often abortive) development programmes. The current generation have top speeds which are equalled (even surpassed) by that of their targets; the American-designed Mark 46, for example, has a speed of 40 knots which is exactly that of the Soviet Alfa class; a stern chase is thus completely out of the question.

The lack of speed and range for torpedoes has been partially answered for surface ships by the use of helicopters and stand-off delivery systems (e.g. ASROC, Ikara) and, in the case of submarines, by SUBROC. There is still, however, a need for a much faster torpedo, which has led to the American-designed Advanced Capability Program (ADCAP) for the Mark 48 torpedo — which will raise the speed to 55 knots — and the British Tigerfish, which is reported to be capable of similar speeds.

The next generation British torpedo, Spearfish, uses a gas turbine and a pump-jet to attain even higher speeds. The Spearfish guidance system is complex. On launch an active/passive sonar transducer operates in the passive mode, changing to active automatically as soon as the target's behaviour indicates that it is aware of the attack. Guidance wires link the torpedo to the launching submarine; not only are commands fed to the torpedo but also sonar information is also passed back.

Warhead design is also becoming more important as submarine hulls become ever stronger, the most difficult target being the enormous double-hulled Soviet Typhoon class SSBN. Some form of directed-energy (hollow-charge) warhead is necessary in such circumstances.

In general terms, the capabilities of current torpedoes lag behind those of the sonars that support them, being slow, lacking in range, noisy and frequently unreliable. There were several reports from the Falklands War that the Argentine Navy suffered from malfunctioning torpedoes, although more recent evidence suggests that some opportunities may have been wasted by launching torpedoes at greater than the recommended firing depth.

Some development work is being done on electric-powered torpedoes, but at the moment although these are quiet, they are also slow and lacking in range. Increases in either can only be obtained by more battery power, which means bigger torpedoes or a smaller warhead. Torpedo sonar, too, needs to be improved and a US Defense Advanced Projects Agency (DARPA) programme is working on this, possibly leading to a torpedo with on-board signal processing, coupled with an interactive fibreoptic link with the parent submarine. A further project is to adopt such a system for use with ASW aircraft, utilising a fibreoptic link from the torpedo to a buoy which has a radio uplink to the launching aircraft.

Below: Standard British launcher, fitted to all destroyers and frigates, is the STWS.1, launching Stingray, Mk 44 or Mk 46 torpedoes.

Above: A vital adjunct in the ASW battle is the torpedo-armed helicopter: this SH-2F LAMPS I is launching a Mk 46 torpedo.

Below: The torpedo has replaced depth-charges and mortars as the most effective anti-submarine weapon for use by surface warships.

Anti-Ship Missiles (ASM)

Naval forces have developed missiles for both offensive and defensive purposes for many years. The first significant demonstration of ASM effectiveness, as we saw earlier, was in 1967 when the Israeli destroyer *Eilat* was sunk by an SS-N-2 missile fired by an Egyptian Navy FAC. That impression was reinforced in 1982 when Argentine naval aircraft used French Exocet missiles in attacks on modern, well-equipped British warships, leading to the sinking of HMS *Coventry*. Despite world-wide publicity generated by this loss and, later, that of the merchant ship *Atlantic Conveyor* a sober assessment indicates that more Exocets were foiled than achieved hits, and that the later hit on HMS *Glamorgan* (from a land-based launcher) did only very limited damage.

In its ship-borne form Exocet is used by many navies and since the Falklands War Exocets have been used in the Middle East Gulf War with a number of very large merchant ships being hit. However, none has sunk nor even been put totally out of action.

The Exocet, like many other current ASMs is subsonic and the new generation of fast-reaction SAMs and CIWS guns should be able to defeat such attacks under most circumstances. However, the latest ASMs such as the Soviet SS-N-19 have speeds of up to Mach 2.5 and may well strain current defence systems beyond their limits. An incoming Exocet flying at a height of 7 to 10ft (2 to 3m) and a speed of Mach 0.9 + should be detected by a frigate's surveillance radar at a range of about 10nm (18.5km), i.e. approximately 60 seconds before impact. Radar tracking would be initiated at a range of 3.4nm (6.3km) (20 seconds to go), and a missile such as Seawolf launched when the incoming ASM was 2nm (3.74km) distant (about 10 to 13 seconds before impact). This is a short enough timescale and requires computer control; indeed, it was reported from the Falklands War that the first time ships' crews became aware of an attack was when the Sea Wolf missiles were launched; without the computer that would have been just

too late! If, however, the missile was an SS-N-19 travelling at Mach 2.5 and at the same sea-skimming height, the distances and timings would be very different, first acquisition at 10nm (18.5km) being just 19 seconds before impact.

Soviet Kirov class battlecruisers mount 20 SS-N-19 ASMs in vertical launch tubes on the foredeck, while Soviet cruisers tend to mount their ASMs in deck-mounted tubes set at about a 20 degree angle; in neither case does it appear that reloading at sea is possible. The SS-N-19 has an estimated range of some 310 miles (500km) and a speed in the region of Mach 2.5. External target detection and designation from aircraft is probably combined with on-board inertial guidance and homing systems.

The US Navy's principal ASM, RGM-84A Harpoon, is somewhat different. It has a turbojet cruise engine and its flight profile is much lower than that of the SS-N-19, but with a final manoeuvre phase to evade CIWS defences. No data inputs are required from the ship after launch and a computer guides the missile to the vicinity of the target where a frequency-agile homing radar takes over for the final phase.

ASMs now form an essential part of the armament of most surface warships. However, it is worth noting that no fleet action, nor even a full-scale ship-to-ship ASM engagement, has yet taken place in a final proof of the systems.

Above: Royal Navy Lynx helicopter armed with four Sea Skua anti-ship missiles. Sea Skua has a range of 16,400 yd (15,000m) and was used with great success in the Falklands War.

Left: The US Harpoon all-weather cruise-missile is one of the most successful of its generation. It can be launched by aircraft, submarines or a surface warship. Range is "over 60nm".

Below: The Norwegian Penguin missile exists in ship- and helicopter-launched versions. Speed is Mach 0.8 and its 264lb (120kg) warhead is effective against any surface target.

Surface-to-Air Missiles (SAM)

Long-range systems

The most sophisticated contemporary air defence system is the US Navy's Aegis, which is based on the AN/SPY-1A multi-function phased-array radar and uses the Standard SM-2 missile. The Standard SM-2 has a monopulse receiver, an inertial reference unit for mid-course guidance, a two-way telemetry link for missile-position reporting, target position updating and guidance correction, and an on-board digital computer. The inertial reference unit enables the missile to navigate itself to the vicinity of the target where the semi-active radar head takes over. SM-2 is able to take full advantage of the Aegis multiple-target capability. This system is currently at sea in the US Navy's Ticonderoga class cruisers, and, in a slightly simplified form (AN/SPY-1D), will be used in the US Navy's Arleigh Burke and the Japanese Maritime Self-Defense Force ''Improved Hatakaze'' class DDGs.

Current major long-range Soviet Navy SAMs are SA-N-6 and SA-N-7. SA-N-6 is a naval version of the land-based SA-10 and has a range of up to 90,000ft (27,432m). The missiles are installed in eight-missile rotating magazines with vertical launchers; there are 12 launchers on Kirov class battlecruisers and eight launchers on Slava class cruisers. SA-N-7 uses a single-arm launcher, with 20 missiles in a below-decks magazine. The Mach 3 missile, a naval version of SA-11, has a range of 30,622 yards (28,000m) and a ceiling of 46,000ft (14,000m). This system has so far only been seen on Sovremenny class destroyers.

Short-range systems

One of the most advanced short-range anti-missile systems is the British Sea Wolf, which can be installed in warships of as little as 1,000 tons displacement. The entire operational sequence is automatic and is timed in milliseconds. Sea Wolf has destroyed an incoming 4.5in shell during tests but, more importantly, it did very well under actual combat conditions in the Falklands War. Sea Wolf is currently deployed in six- or four-

canister launch units with manual reloading (presumably to avoid the weight and complexity of an automatic system) and is also available in a twin standard ISO 6m container installation. A vertical launch installation is under development.

The Soviet Navy has a plethora of short-range missile systems. SA-N-4 has been in service for 20 years and is installed in numerous classes of ship ranging from Kirov class battlecruisers (28,000 tons) to Sarancha class hydrofoils (320 tons). The twin-arm launcher retracts into a 20-round magazine in an extremely neat and compact installation. The missile has a range of 9,800 yards (9,000m) and an operational envelope of 30 to 10,000ft (9 to 3,050m) in the air defence role. It has a secondary anti-ship capability.

SA-N-5 and SA-N-8 are naval versions of SA-7 and its successor SA-14, respectively. SA-N-5 is fitted in small combatants (e.g. corvettes, FAC),

landing ships and auxiliaries. The IR-homing, visually-aimed missile is launched from either a 4-missile rack, which includes the operator, or from a shoulder-tube. Range is 4,812 yards (4,400m) and ceiling 7,800ft (2,377m). SA-N-8 uses identical launchers as SA-N-5 but with a new missile with a head-on targetting capability.

The US Navy short-range air-defence missile is the Sea Sparrow (RIM-7), formerly known as the basic point defense missile system (BPDMS). These missiles are fired from an 8-round Mark 29 launcher and are mounted in such disparate types as Nimitz class carriers and Sacramento class replenishment ships. Using semi-active radar homing (SARH) the missile has a range of 8nm (15km). It is also in wide-scale service as NATO Sea Sparrow with many NATO navies. A replacement system, the rolling airframe missile (RAM), is under development and should enter service in the early-1990s.

Left: USS *Bunker Hill* was the first US warship to test the vertical launch system (VLS). Here three test missiles are being fired in sequence from the forward magazine.

Right: Sea Wolf SAM is fired from a 6-cell launcher on board a Royal Navy frigate. The ultra-fast reactions of the Sea Wolf proved extremely effective in the Falklands War.

Below: The Mach 2 + , rolling-airframe missile (RAM), developed jointly by the United States, West Germany and Denmark.

ASW Weapons

Depth charges

The depth charge, the archetypal World War II ASW weapon, is now little used by larger surface ships, since to allow a modern submarine within launcher range, about 2 miles (3.2km), would be very hazardous. However, depth charges are still used by some smaller ASW vessels, such as the Soviet Pauk class FPBs. Depth bombs are used by ASW helicopters; a good example is the British Mark 11 which contains 180lb (81.6kg) of torpex. Far more effective, but with major political implications is the nuclear depth bomb, exemplified by the American B57, which can be deployed on S-3 Viking and P-3 Orion aircraft and SH-3 Sea King helicopters. The B57 weapon has a reported yield in the 5 to 20kT range.

Mines

Mines have a major role in ASW, although the days of the old-fashioned moored or bottom-sitting mine are probably numbered. Far more effective is the US Navy's CAPTOR (CAPsulated TORpedo) which is designed exclusively for attacking submarines. CAPTOR consists of a Mark 46 torpedo housed in a tube which can be laid by submarines, aircraft or surface ships. It sits on the ocean floor and monitors all passing maritime traffic using passive sonar, with a range of some 3,000ft (1,000m), "gated" to exclude surface traffic. Having identified a submarine target the active sonar is switched on, optimum launch time computed and the torpedo launched to home automatically onto the target. As no IFF is fitted, friendly submarines must be kept clear.

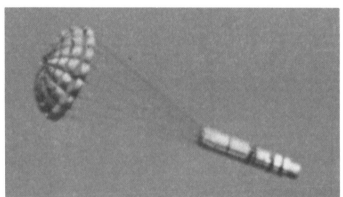

Stand-off weapons

To overcome the problem of reaching the target submarine before it can itself attack its hunter a number of stand-off weapons have been developed which deliver a depth-charge or a torpedo by a carrier missile or rocket. The American ASROC (Anti-Submarine ROCket) consists of a Mark 46 acoustic homing torpedo with a strap-on rocket motor. Similar weapons are produced in France (Malafon), Australia (Ikara) and the USSR (FRAS-1, SS-N-14). Ranges are not great: for example, that of ASROC is estimated to be 1.25 to 6.2 miles (2 to 10km). The US SUBROC (SUBmarine ROCket) and Soviet SS-N-15/16 provide submarines with a similar capability, but in this case they are fired from standard torpedo tubes underwater, before driving to the surface and then into the air.

Clearly a new weapons system to combat the threat posed by very fast and deep diving submarines such as the Soviet Alfa and Sierra classes was needed. A project to replace SUBROC, which was designated as an anti-submarine warfare/stand-off weapon (ASW/SOW), was replaced in 1981 by a project to produce one common system to replace both SUBROC and ASROC. This programme proved abortive and has been replaced by yet another project, the stand-off weapon (SOW) (also known as Sea Lance), which is designed to be launched from Los Angeles class SSNs at up to 80 per cent of their test depths. Estimated range is some 106nm (199km). It is planned to launch Sea Lance from standard 21in (533mm) torpedo tubes and it will carry either nuclear or conventional warheads.

Left: The US CAPTOR mine can be laid by aircraft (as here), surface ships or submarines.

Right: Submarines are detected by sonar, using transducer arrays such as this Plessey PMS-40.

Below Left: The US anti-submarine rocket (ASROC) enables surface ships to attack distant targets.

Below: The Royal Navy Type 2016 sonar is a sophisticated hull-mounted system.

Submarine Weapons

After World War II virtually every submarine abandoned gun armament and for several decades the only weapon available to attack and patrol submarines was the torpedo. In numerous cases, however, very advanced and sophisticated SSNs and SSBNs were at sea with torpedoes which had little better performance than those of World War II. The torpedo has had an extraordinary history in recent years with vast sums being expended by many nations, but, until recently, with little advance in performance or reliability.

We have discussed torpedoes already, and now turn to the submarine's principle underwater weapons, ballistic and cruise missiles.

Below: Tomahawk cruise missiles have given American submarines a new capability, enabling them to carry out conventional attacks against targets deep inland. In this test a Tomahawk launched from a submarine submerged off the Southern Californian coast flew across the shore of San Clemente Island to hit its intended target with devastating precision. In these pictures the Tomahawk approaches the target (1) and the warhead detonates shortly after the nosecone has penetrated the structure (2). The explosion causes a fireball (3), following which the target is totally destroyed (4).

Submarine-launched ballistic missiles (SLBM)

In one of the boldest technological projects in history, the SLBM concept was formulated by Admiral W.F. Rayborn, USN, and a team from Lockheed. The result was Polaris, which reached operational status in November 1960 and changed the nature of strategic deterrence and the face of naval conflict.

All SLBM systems comprise five basic sub-systems. First is the submarine (SSBN) itself which delivers the missiles safely to the launch point. Secondly, the navigational system, which continuously determines the position, velocity and attitude of the submarine. Thirdly, the fire control sub-system, which prepares and fires the missiles in the minimum possible time. Fourthly, the launch sub-system stores, protects and ejects the missile, which, finally, delivers the re-entry vehicle (RV) sub-system. This consists of a bus and a number of warheads containing the nuclear devices, decoys and (in some cases) terminal guidance packages.

Missile warhead accuracy is assessed by the "circular error probable" (cep), the radius of a notional circle, centred upon the point of aim (the target), into which 50 per cent of all warheads launched will fall. (Cep is measured in nautical miles (nm); 1nm = 6,080ft = 1.15 statute miles = 1.852km). For many years SLBM warheads remained fundamentally inaccurate with ceps of 0.25nm (460m) or greater and thus could only be used in a "counter-value role", targetted against cities and other area

targets. However, the predicted entry into service of manoeuvrable re-entry vehicles (MaRVs) with terminal guidance will alter the situation since, for example, the Mark 600 MaRV to be fitted to Trident 2 (D-5) will be capable of a cep of 0.07nm (122m). This creates the possibility that such SLBMs could be used in a counter-force role, i.e. against enemy strategic weapons sites (e.g. ICBM fields), a step with significant implications for the balance of power.

The oldest SLBM in the US Navy inventory is Poseidon (C-3), which is armed with up to 14 MIRV warheads, each with a 50kT yield. Range with 14 warheads is 2,500nm (4,630km) but this is increased to 3,200nm (5,926km) if only ten are carried. Poseidon will continue to equip a number of Lafayette class SSBNS for some years, but numbers are diminishing as boats are decommissioned to comply with SALT-II ceilings as Trident-armed Ohio class SSBNs are commissioned.

Trident-I (C-4) was designed to have a similar payload and accuracy to Poseidon (C-3), but much greater range to allow the use of larger patrol areas. The Trident-I (C-4) design requirement emphasised range. The fitting of an "aerospike", which extends after launch, creates the same aerodynamic effect as a sharp, slender nose, reducing drag by some 50 per cent. Allied to a third-stage motor and improved fuel, this gives a range of 4,230nm (7,833km) at full payload (i.e. eight Mark 4 RVs with W-76 warheads, 100kT yield): more with reduced payload. The Mark 5

navigation system incorporates in-flight updating for the inertial navigation system (INS), in which a stellar sensor takes a star sight during the post-boost phase, which is used to correct the flight path. As a result Trident-I (C-4) has a reported cep of 0.25nm (457m), which may be reduced to 0.12nm (229m) in future.

Trident II (D-5) is designed to have even greater accuracy. As a result it is longer, 45.8ft (13.96m) compared to 34.08ft (10.4m), with slightly increased diameter, 74.4in (1.89m) compared to 74in (1.9m). It is capable of carrying 14 RVs, but the SALT-II limits this to ten. The Mark 5 RV has a yield of 475kT and a cep of 0.19nm (122m), but the Mark 600 MaRV may be carried in due course to reduce the chances of interception. The Mark 5 RV is quoted as designed to take different warheads "tailored to the target assignment". The Trident-II (D- 5) will equip 20 US Navy Ohio class SSBNs (24 missiles each) and the four new Royal Navy SSBNs (16 missiles each).

Latest Soviet Navy SLBMs are SS-N-20 on the Typhoon class and SS-N-23 on the Delta IV. Little is known of SS-N-23 except that, somewhat surprisingly, it is liquid-fuelled, and that it has greater throw-weight and accuracy than SS-N-18 fitted to Delta III SSBNs; it carries up to seven MIRVs. SS-N-20 is a three-stage solid-fuel missile with a design range of 4,800nm (8,890km), carrying six to nine RVs; cep is 0.35nm (640m). On October 21, 1982 a Typhoon class SSBN launched four SS-N-20s simultaneously, a significant develop-

ment, since, in all other known cases, missiles must be launched sequentially with some 1 to 2 minutes between each.

There are a number of other, older Soviet SLBMs still in service. Oldest is SS-N-6 in Yankee I submarines, a 1,600nm (2,963km) range missile with two large-yield MRVs. This very old system (it entered service in 1968) is being withdrawn as new SSBNs join the fleet, to comply with SALT-II. It was a fire in one of these missiles which led to the sinking of a Yankee I off the US coast in 1987. The sole Yankee II carries SS-N-17, a curiosity in the Soviet armoury, as it is only carried by this one boat; why it remains in service has never become clear. SS-N-8, with a single 1.5mT warhead and a cep of 1nm (1,500m) (and thus clearly capable only of a counter-value role) equips Delta I and Delta II SSBNs. SS-N-18 is deployed on Delta III. This is a two-stage missile with three versions: Mod 1, three 200kT MRV; Mod 2, one 450kT RV; Mod 3, seven 200kT MIRVs.

Other nations with SSBN/SLBM systems are Britain, France and the People's Republic of China. Current British SLBMs are Polaris A-3TK missiles, which were re-motored in the early-1980s, and have a new front-end of entirely British origin, designated Chevaline. Each missile is reported to carry six 40kT MRVs. The older French SSBNs carry the M-20 missile, but the latest boats to join the fleet carry the new M-4 missile with six 150kT MIRVs. The Chinese SSBNs, of which at least two are in service, are armed with 12 CSS-N-3 SLBM.

Submarine-launched cruise missiles (SLCM)

Submarine-launched cruise missiles (SLCM) have been in service for many years and the Soviet Navy has long had specialised boats to carry them. Juliett class diesel-electric, cruise-missile submarines (SSG) and nuclear-powered boats (SSGN) (Echo, Charlie and Oscar classes) carry SLCM mounted in bins, either amidships or in the bows. The missiles (SS-N-3, -7, -9 and -19) can be launched from underwater and have ranges up to 600 miles (966km); their most probable role is in attacking NATO task groups in the North Atlantic, especially those formed around attack aircraft carriers.

The US Navy took a different approach and produced weapons to be launched from standard 21in (533mm) torpedo tubes. This was applied to the Sub-Harpoon anti-ship missile and Tomahawk anti-ship (T-ASM) and land attack (T-LAM) missile, but, after vast expenditure on the Tomahawk programme, it was realised that the missiles would take up too much valuable space in the torpedo rooms. It has, therefore, been decided to fit them in vertically-mounted tubes inside the upper casing between the bow sonar and the forward end of the pressure hull. This is a significant capability enhancement at little cost, but it is now irrelevant as to whether the missile can fit a torpedo tube or not, and thus much R&D money and effort has been wasted. Harpoon can attack ships out to "over 60nm (84km)" and the T-ASM to 250nm (400km), while the T-LAM has a range

Below: Weapons now available to submarines include torpedoes for use against surface ships and other submarines, as well as cruise-missiles for use against naval or land targets.

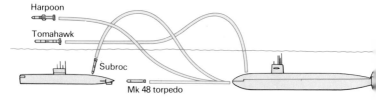

Harpoon

Tomahawk

Subroc

Mk 48 torpedo

of 1,400nm (2,100km), and has both conventional and nuclear warheads. The main problem with T-LAM is that to exploit its capabilities fully it needs external target information and a system known as Outlaw Shark is being deployed to achieve this. The deployment of Tomahawk in this role has, however, increased the need for two-way communications with sub-marines, a notoriously difficult problem.

The only other submarine-launched anti-ship missile is the French SM-39 Exocet. This is a new version of the very successful ship-launched MM-38 missile. Launched from a standard 21in (533mm) torpedo tube SM-39 has a range of over 27nm (50km).

Above: This submarine-launched US Trident I missile epitomises the immense strategic power now exercised by submarines.

Below: Despite the advent of other weapons systems, torpedoes remain of vital importance to the submariner.

Task Forces

The major operational consideration of a naval commander-in-chief is the deployment of his fleet at sea. Until the end of World War II warships were formed into battle fleets, consisting in some cases of several hundred warships operating together. Even today similar principles apply, with a number of warships being grouped together in a balanced force to provide a complementary offensive capability and mutual protection. These are usually designated battle groups or task forces. The two basic types of battle group currently deployed by the major navies are carrier battle groups (CVBG) and battleships battle groups (BBBG). Which type is used — and the detailed composition of each — depends upon a combination of factors, the most important of which are the mission, the threat and the resources available.

Once at sea, a battle group has to protect itself against several sources of attack and protective screens are created around the main body. Individual ships are so positioned that the characteristics of their weapons systems can best be exploited for the benefit of the group as a whole. To ensure the maximum protection for the highest value warships the commander must take into account the threat, its nature and likely direction, and the strengths and weaknesses of the units within the force. All of these must be deployed and organised to provide protection against air (both aircraft and missiles), surface and sub-surface attack, and to allow the battle group to carry out its assigned mission.

The commander is faced with reconciling a number of contradictory factors. For example, when faced with the possibility of tactical nuclear attack it is clearly essential for him to disperse his ships as widely as possible so that, in the event of such an attack, as few ships as possible are damaged. On the other hand, the most effective air defence is achieved by concentrating units to give the maximum firepower of both missiles and guns over the highest value defending units.

Right: USS *Long Beach*, a nuclear-powered cruiser, and USS *Bunker Hill*, a conventionally-powered Ticonderoga class cruiser, on patrol in the Gulf. This international operation was a very successful example of the controlled use of seapower.

Below: A US carrier task group at sea is an awesome concentration of fire power. The carrier has some 85 aircraft embarked, whose capabilities cover the entire spectrum from fighters and attack types, through AEW and ASW to ECM and tankers. The carrier is escorted by a Ticonderoga class cruiser equipped with the Aegis air defence system and four frigates and destroyers for ASW defence. Finally, the whole group is supported by two replenishment vessels carrying supplies of fuel, ammunition, stores and food.

Surface Warfare

An essential element of naval surface warfare is to locate and identify the enemy. This appears to be a simplistic statement and it might appear that, with the plethora of intelligence-gathering and sensor systems now available, this would be an easy task. Such is not, however, the case and fleets still have considerable difficulty, first, in finding each other and, subsequently, in making positive identification of individual targets.

For example, modern naval missiles have such long ranges that an external means of identification and guidance is frequently required. The primary anti-ship weapon of the Soviet Kirov class battlecruisers is SS-N-19 with a range of 300nm (500km), which is far outside current radar coverage. Targets thus have to be acquired and identified by external sources, such as Tu-16 Badger-F reconnaissance and ELINT aircraft, or Hormone-B reconnaissance helicopters, or forward-positioned submarines. The difficulties are compounded in that, in carrying out such reconnaissance, these units may themselves be detected by the enemy, thus giving away not only the existence of a threat, but possibly its direction, as well.

In a "real-life" example, during the early stages of the Falklands War, both British and Argentinian surface groups were at sea, but they had the greatest difficulty in finding each other. Then, later in the campaign, identification was still not always accurate, as, for example, when Argentine Navy Super Etendard strike aircraft sank the support ship *Atlantic Conveyor* under the impression that she was either HMS *Hermes* or HMS *Illustrious*; i.e., one of the two critical British aircraft carriers.

For the surface units themselves their primary source of target information is radar, which normally has a range of some 40 to 60nm (74 to 111km). Radar has, however, two drawbacks. First, it does not currently have a means of positively identifying a target, which offers an obvious opportunity for deception. For example, an aircraft carrier's position may be concealed by placing a lower-value unit with a similar radar signature (e.g. a replenishment oiler or a container ship) where the carrier might be expected to be; this risks the former's loss, but protects the carrier. Another method of confusing the enemy could be to divide the battle group into several sub-groups, so that it is unclear which contains the high-value ships. The second major problem with radar is that it is an active electronic device, which means that it can be monitored by hostile EW devices, thus compromising the fleet's position.

There is, in fact, a major conflict going on in the invisible, but nevertheless crucial, area of the electronic spectrum. Electronic countermeasures

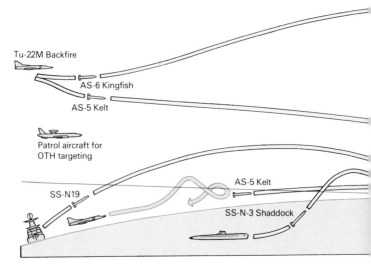

(ECM) are used to deceive the enemy and to deny him essential target information. For example, radar transmissions can be protected (at least partially) by electronic techniques such as frequency hopping, which are known collectively as electronic counter-countermeasures (ECCM). Further, jamming an opponent's radar frequencies may deny him essential range information, while during the final stages of a missile attack chaff can be used to distort the apparent position of the task group or of an individual ship. Deception, too, has a role to play. During the Falklands War, for example, as the British Task Force approached the islands a destroyer was positioned well to the east to transmit radio and radar signals as a decoy to the shadowing Argentinian reconnaissance aircraft.

Above: For surface warships most target information comes from radar systems.

Below: The Soviet missile threat to a NATO surface warship is impressive, ranging from aircraft-launched AS-5 and AS-6 through ship-launched SS-N-19 to submarine-launched SS-N-9. The hazard for the defence is increased by the growing number of missiles using the sea-skimming mode to minimise radar-warning time. The problem is compounded by the effects of the Earth's curvature on a ship's radar horizon, which enables attacking aircraft to approach beneath the defender's radar.

Above: The US Harpoon is one of many anti-ship missile systems now in service around the world.

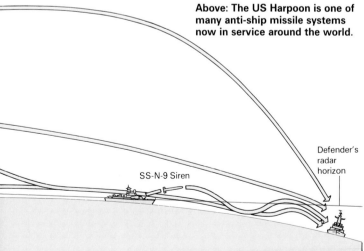

SS-N-9 Siren

Defender's radar horizon

Anti-Air Warfare

Anti-air warfare (AAW) covers defence against both aircraft and missiles, and AAW tactics are based upon the concept of defence in depth. Ideally, the attacker should itself be destroyed far from the battle group before it can compute a weapon launch solution. Assuming that this has not happened, defence against incoming aircraft or missiles starts with an outer air battle and continues through successive combat regions, with engagement of approaching "hostiles" taking place in each

This process seeks to achieve progressive attrition of air attacks and at best eliminate, or at worst reduce, them to manageable proportions by the time they reach the final zone of point defence of individual ships.

Early warning of air attack is essential. Military intelligence reports and satellite surveillance provide strategic warning of the existence of a threat, but neither is likely to provide timely warning once a hostile attack is underway. For this the only real answer is an airborne early warning (AEW) aircraft patrolling at an adequate distance from the fleet. The US Navy's

Below: The positioning of the air defence ships in a task force is determined by the range of their missile systems, with the underlying principle being, again, that of defence in depth. In this example, the main body is an aircraft carrier with an escorting cruiser. The first-line of air defence is provided by air defence ships with medium-range and area defence SAM systems. Closer in, most ships have self-defence systems, whilst at the centre the cruiser uses its guns, short-range missiles and CIWS to supplement those of the carrier. These defences are, of course, integrated with the carrier's own fighter aircraft.

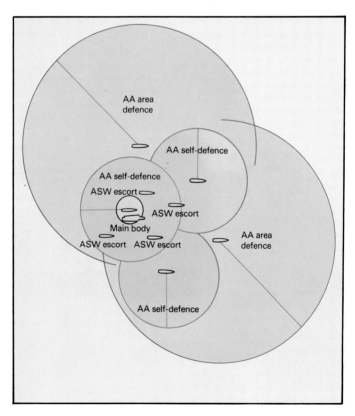

E-2C Hawkeye AEW aircraft, flying at a height of 30,000ft (9,000m) can increase the surface coverage of a force out to 260nm (480km); it can also track up to 800 targets and control up to 40 intercepts simultaneously.

If a naval force has no carrier and no AEW aircraft then the only alternative is a radar-picket ship, equipped with a long-range, high-definition radar, such as the American-designed SPS-40, British Type 965R, or Soviet Top Pair. Positioned near the edge of the battle group's radar horizon, a typical radar picket ship can extend radar surface coverage by a further 60nm (111km) and air coverage by up to about 200nm (371km), although the latter is very susceptible to climatic conditions. However, despite increasing a task force's radar coverage, such radar pickets are themselves vulnerable to air attack. This was shown only too clearly during the Falklands War when the British task force, due to the scrapping of the final fleet carrier just a few years earlier, had no AEW aircraft. This was instrumental in the losses suffered by the Royal Navy, especially that of HMS *Sheffield* on May 4, 1982 to an air-launched missile.

Above: The Falklands War showed that one of the most vital needs of a task force is airborne early warning, provided by aircraft such as this US Grumman E-2C Hawkeye. The Soviet and French navies will both need such a type to protect their new nuclear carriers.

Below: A Grumman F-14 Tomcat is seen here firing a Hughes AIM-54C Phoenix missile, which provides air defence over an area exceeding 12,000 square miles (31,000km²) from sea level to high altitude.

Anti-Submarine Warfare (ASW)

Of all the types of modern naval warfare it is ASW that most occupies the thinking of naval strategists and tacticians. A task-force commander must, as in AAW defence, seek to establish a multi-layered defence in depth, optimising the use of each unit's specialisation. The task force will receive external inputs to its ASW plot, particularly from strategic ASW systems such as undersea barriers (e.g. the American SOSUS) and satellite surveillance systems. Ultimately, however, defence of the task group is the responsibility of the commander.

The main body proceeds on a zigzag course maintaining an overall speed in the required direction of advance of only some 10 knots. To ensure that each area is properly sanitised and to enable effective control to be exercised, each unit and helicopter is allocated a specific sector, normally some 60 to 72nm² (110 to 135km²) in area, to defend. Each ship manoeuvres continuously to deny attacking submarines the information they need to set up an attacking solution for their weapons systems. Ships use mainly hull-mounted sonars, usually in the active mode, and larger units (such as carriers) tow noise-making anti-torpedo decoys.

Outside this inner zone the next area is patrolled by ships and aircraft using passive sonar devices, particularly towed arrays, such as the American TACTAS. Helicopters also operate in this zone, but using passive sonobuoys. Friendly hunter-killer SSNs are also allocated specific areas, where they can use their ASW sensors and weapons systems to maximum effect, well clear of the noise of cavitating propellers and where they can safely assume that any movement detected is hostile.

Yet further out is the outer screen, where, well in advance of the main body, are the LRMP aircraft, utilising the full range of their detection devices — radar, sonobuoys MAD and visual observation.

Below: Sonar is still the only effective means of detecting submerged submarines. This is a "dunking" sonar array of a type used by many ASW helicopters.

Right: Royal Navy Sea King HAS-2 ASW helicopter. The deployment of such helicopters in frigates and destroyers has revolutionised their ASW capabilities.

Below: Soviet Ilyushin Il-38 May land-based ASW and maritime patrol aircraft, on patrol over the Indian Ocean.

The Carrier Battle Group (CVBG)

Currently, and for the foreseeable future, the most powerful instrument of naval seapower is the aircraft carrier battle group (CVBG). With a properly balanced air wing and with the necessary mix of warships, such a group can have a unique four-dimensional capability against air, surface, land and underwater targets at ranges of many hundreds of miles.

In the US Navy such a CVBG might comprise: one aircraft carrier, two cruisers (of which at least one would be Aegis-equipped), at least one nuclear-powered submarine, four general-purpose destroyers (e.g. Spruance or Arleigh Burke class) and four ASW frigates (Oliver Hazard Perry class). There would also be a Sacramento class fast replenishment ship and a fleet oiler, probably of either the Cimmaron or Wichita class. In a high-threat situation an Iowa class battleship might also form part of the CVBG to enhance the group's anti-surface capabilities.

Despite the possible presence of a battleship, the greatest strength in such a group is its well-balanced carrier air wing, with its capability for AEW, ASW, CAP and, above all, long-range strike. The air power available is awesome. There are minor variations in the total number of aircraft carried on board the various classes of US Navy super-carrier, but a typical air wing comprises a total of 78 fixed-wing and 8 rotary-wing aircraft:

E-2Cs and S-3As make it possible to detect hostile ships, aircraft or submarines at long-range and thus for them to be attacked and destroyed before they can threaten friendly units. The Soviet Navy appears to have recognised this and is developing a much larger and more capable type of carrier (the Kremlin class), but they will also have to develop the offensive and defensive types of carrier-borne aircraft as well, to make these ships a viable tactical proposition.

Powerful as these carriers are, particularly in the case of the US Navy, it would be wrong to overlook their vulnerability. In most circumstances they are the highest value naval units in a conflict and must, therefore, inevitably be at the top of an enemy's target list. Despite the fighters carried aboard the carrier and the air defence missile systems of the escorts it is always possible that an air strike could fight its way through for a direct attack on a carrier. Far more likely, however, is an over-the-horizon attack by air-, ship-, or submarine-launched missiles, probably from several different directions simultaneously to saturate the defences. Alternatively, an underwater attack is highly possible, and an aircraft carrier makes a very large and relatively slow manouevring target for a submarine captain. Finally, in a nuclear war the carriers might well be targetted by land-based missiles, and there have been reports that some of the older Soviet ICBMs may have been allocated such a role.

All-Weather Fighters	Grumman F-14 Tomcat	20
Attack	McDonnell Douglas F/A-18 Hornet	18
Electronic Warfare	Grumman EA-6B Prowler	5
Attack	Grumman A-6E Intruder	20
Airborne Early Warning	Grumman E-2C Hawkeye	5
Long-range ASW	Lockheed S-3A Viking	10
Short-range ASW	Boeing-Vertol SH-3D Sea King	8
		86

To obtain the greatest effectiveness from this force it must be used offensively. First, it enables the commander to carry out long-range strikes with either nuclear or conventional weapons against land or naval targets using the A-6Es and F/A-18s, protected by the EA-6Bs and fighters (F-14s or F/A-18s). Secondly, the

These super-carriers are extremely expensive in themselves with a further vast expense for the associated air wings of specialised naval aircraft. This has simply priced a number of navies, even one as large as the British Royal Navy, out of the market. This has given rise to another type of carrier battle group, the CVG, whose role is

Above: Carrier battle group (CVBG) at sea; USS *Midway* (CV 41) is escorted by five warships and an oiler. Even such a small (by US standards) carrier has the airpower of a medium-sized force.

Below: Typical disposition of a Soviet task force. The main body — carrier *Minsk* and battlecruiser *Kirov* — changes course every few minutes to reduce the threat posed by submarines. Outlying escorts constantly patrol sectors 60-72 square miles (155-189km²) guarding the main body against air and submarine attack. Such a group can advance at relatively high speed towards its objective, despite alterations of course in an ASW environment being frequent. The positions of the escort ships are determined by the capabilities of their detection and weapons systems. If one ship is released, the sectors of the remainder must be adjusted.

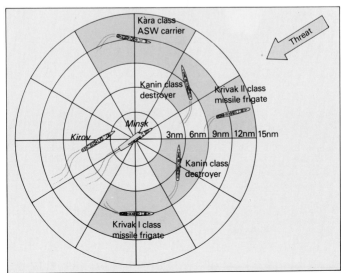

primarily ASW, centred on a somewhat smaller carrier, such as the British Invincible class, the Italian Garibaldi class and Spanish Principe de Asturia class. These carriers can form an ASW CVG in general war, deploying an air wing of ASW helicopters and V/STOL fighters, or they could deploy in a strike role in limited war. The mix of aircraft types can, of course, be varied to suit the mission and aircraft such as the Harrier/Sea Harrier and the larger ASW helicopters can carry ASMs to give a long-range anti-ship capability. The value of these smaller carriers was amply proven during the Falklands War, where the carriers *Hermes* and *Invincible* were absolutely essential to the success of the British campaign.

Such carriers would form the central element of an ASW CVG and would have a vital role in keeping sea lanes open in general war. This is effectively the concept of "sea control" proposed by Admiral Zumwalt, US Chief of Navy Operations in the early 1970s. They would deploy with a mix of escorting destroyers and frigates, with at least one replenishment ship in company and, in the case of the Royal Navy, probably one or more SSNs in support. However, such CVBGs lack an integral AEW capability, although the Royal Navy has attempted to overcome this by converting a small number of Sea King

helicopters to the AEW role.

A further type of carrier is appearing which is similar in role to the small ASW carriers described above, but much larger in size. The US Navy's Wasp class is convertible from the assault ship role to that of an ASW carrier, in which role it would carry 20 AV-8B Harrier V/STOL aircraft and six SH-60B ASW helicopters.

The second of these larger types is the Soviet Kiev class (43,000 tons). A current Soviet Navy CVBG might comprise: one Kiev class carrier, a Kirov class battlecruiser, four general-purpose destroyers (Sovremenny class), four ASW destroyers (Udaloy class), at least one SSN, possibly several SSGNs (Oscar or Charlie class) and at least one replenishment ship (Berezina or Boris Chilikin class). This is a powerful force, but the capability of the air wing does not start to approach that of the US Navy's CVBG as the Kiev class only currently carry twelve Yak-38 Forger V/STOL fighters and up to 17 Ka-27 Helix ASW helicopters. A particular weakness is the lack of AEW and long-range ASW aircraft, which would give a Soviet commander the same problems as those faced by the British task force in the South Atlantic in 1982. Indeed, this is not a strike group in the sense of an American CVBG, but an ASW group with an enhanced anti-surface capability (particularly if a Kirov class battlecruiser is present).

Above: The tote boards in a US aircraft carrier's operations centre give an instant analysis of the status of the carrier air group and of every aircraft and crew it possesses.

Below Left: The French Navy retains an effective carrier capability, currently centred upon the *Foch* and *Clemenceau*, but in the mid-1990s the latter will be replaced by the nuclear-powered *Charles de Gaulle*.

Below: Soviet naval capabilities made a dramatic advance when the Kiev class aircraft carriers joined the fleet in the 1970s. They, too, can now despatch carrier battle groups to distant trouble spots.

The Battleship Battle Group (BBBG)

In the US Navy the major alternative to the CVBG is the battleship battle group (BBBG). As with any other type of battle group, the composition of a BBBG would be tailored to the mission and tactical situation, but the planned "normal" composition of a BBBG is likely to be: one Iowa class battleship, one Ticonderoga class (CG 47) Aegis guided-missile cruiser, three Arleigh Burke (DDG 51) destroyers and at least one RAS ship, probably a Wichita class replenishment oiler (AOR). The DDG 51s will not be available until 1991/2 and until then other types of destroyer and frigate will be used. At least one SSN is likely to be in support of the BBBG in general war, but in lower-threat situations such a presence might not be necessary.

Probably the most important single mission for a BBBG is to operate in an offensive role in conjunction with CVBGs in a high-threat environment. A single-carrier CVBG could be reinforced by a BBBG, but the most potent combination of all is a BBBG added to a two-carrier CVBG. Comprising two carriers, a battleship, two or three Aegis cruisers, ten to 15 destroyers or frigates and several SSNs, this group (possibly better described as a "battle fleet") would pose any potential enemy with a tactical problem insoluble by any means other than a multi-weapon nuclear strike.

In a high-threat environment it would clearly be dangerous for a BBBG to operate without the air cover provided by a CVBG, despite the air defence provided by the Aegis cruiser and the other escorts, and the battleship's own constructional robustness. However, it may well frequently be possible for BBBGs to operate independently and in medium- and low-threat situations their tasks could include offensive operations against hostile naval surface forces, using either missiles or guns, depending upon the range and the tactical environment. A BBBG is capable of hitting hostile naval warships far over-the-horizon using its Tomahawk and Harpoon missiles and at closer ranges — up to 47,000 yards (42,977m) — with its main 16in (406mm) guns, and there is no warship afloat capable of withstanding that type of fire.

The BBBG could also be used in support of amphibious operations, a role which the Iowas (and other, older battleships, long since scrapped) performed so well in World War II. In such a role, the Iowa-based BBBG provides an amphibious force with cover against surface and air attack, and can

Below: Ships capable of firing at inland targets offer ideal support for ground forces. Iowa class battleships' 16in (406mm) guns have a maximum range of 23.6 miles (38,000m), with guidance given by ground or airborne spotters.

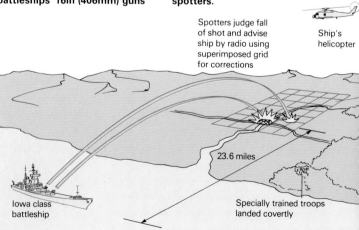

Spotters judge fall of shot and advise ship by radio using superimposed grid for corrections

Ship's helicopter

23.6 miles

Iowa class battleship

Specially trained troops landed covertly

also bombard targets ashore in support of the landings. In the latter role the 16in (406mm) guns of the Iowa class have a degree of accuracy, response-time and penetrating capability unmatched by any contemporary air-delivered weapon.

Finally, in peacetime the BBBG can perform the task of "showing the flag" in an impressive way which no other type of ship can really equal. This can be both in the friendliest sense or to establish an "offshore presence" to restore calm.

It would be feasible for the Soviet Navy to form a BBBG, based upon the Kirov class battlecruisers. These, too, are large and impressive-looking ships, with a heavy armament and great endurance. As with US Navy BBBGs, the Kirovs would be accompanied by a balanced force of cruisers and destroyers to give AAW and ASW protection. There are, however, major differences. First, the Kirovs do not possess a heavy gun armament (the *Kirov*, first of class, mounts two single 100mm guns, while the later units mount one twin 130mm turret apiece), and neither bears any comparison with the nine mighty 16in (406mm) guns of the Iowas. Secondly, the Kirovs are built to modern "light" specifications, with scant armour protection and their survivability is poor in comparison with the Iowas.

Above: USS *New Jersey* (BB 62) Surface Action Group transits Hawaiian waters en route from South-East Asia to Central America.

Below: The Soviet *Kirov* appeared forty years after the US Navy's Iowa class battleships, but her mission is the same: control of the seas.

Command, Control and Communications (C³)

Command, control and communications (C³) are essential to a battle group and, as any visual inspection of the multiplicity of antennas on the upper works of a modern warship will show, a great range of communications systems is required. Such systems include high-frequency (HF), for long-range links and distress frequencies, very high frequency (VHF) to ultra-high frequency (UHF) for line-of-sight paths within the battle group, and between ships and aircraft, to super high frequency (SHF) for satellite communications.

For example, the Iowa class battleships carry OE-82 satellite links, using two 8ft (2.44m) dish antennas; one is mounted on a platform on the after-side of the second stack and the other

Right: The combat information centre (CIC) aboard a Spruance class destroyer, with the Plotter manager (seated) overseeing the activities being conducted as part of the naval tactical data system (NTDS). The plethora of electronic weapons control, communications and sensor systems aboard modern warships is creating growing problems of control and coordination, and old-fashioned manual methods are being replaced by automated data management systems. However, human operators and controllers remain in command. One of the lessons of the Falklands War was that CICs such as this one are vulnerable and must be given armour protection as well as being duplicated.

on the air defence level on the foretop. One of the most important systems aboard is the naval tactical data system (NTDS), the large discone/cage antenna for which is sited prominently on the battleship's bows. NTDS incorporates various data links, such as the NATO standardised Links 11 and 14.

Link 11 is a crypto-secure weapons direction system which provides a two-way flow of target information between NTDS-equipped ships and a one-way link of target information to non-NTDS equipped ships. (At present the Iowas have a Link 11 receive-only capability for the Tomahawk weapons control system.) Link 14 provides for the transfer of selected data from an NTDS computer to a teleprinter on a non-NTDS ship, which is then used to transfer the information manually to a plotting table. All four Iowas have Link 14.

Left: An old-fashioned control centre with a seaman marking the tactical situation on a transparent tote board with a chinagraph crayon. Such methods are still used in many ships, but are no longer adequate for modern warfare. Ships must not only control their own systems, but must also coordinate them with those in other ships in the task group and manual methods just cannot cope any longer. Automatic data processing (ADP) is being brought in to help and is producing a discipline of its own, known as "Command, Control and Communications" or "C³". ADP is being used not just within ships, but also to exchange data between ships in the same group, and also between ships and shore facilities.

Nimitz Class

Origin: United States.

Displacement: CVN-68 to -70: 72,798 tons light; 93,900 tons full load. CVN-71 to -75: 73,973 tons light; 96,836 tons full load.

Dimensions: CVN-68 to -70: Length overall 1,073 ft (327.0m); beam 134ft (40.85m); draught 37ft (11.3m). CVN-71 to -75: Length overall 1,092ft (332.85m); beam 134ft (40.85m); draught 38.42ft (11.71m).

Propulsion: 2 pressurised water-cooled A4W/A1G nuclear reactors; 4 geared steam turbines; 280,000shp; 4 shafts.

Performance: 30 plus knots.

Built: 1968 to 1997.

Ships: Nimitz class — *Nimitz* (CVN 68), *Dwight D Eisenhower* (CVN 69), *Carl Vinson* (CVN 70). Improved Nimitz class — *Theodore Roosevelt* (CVN 71), *Abràham Lincoln* (CVN 72), *George Washington* (CVN 73) (fitting out).

Complement: Ship's crew — 569 officers, 3,091 ratings. Aviation — 304 officers, 2,322 ratings.

Armament: 3 Mark 29 Sea Sparrow launchers (24 missiles). 4 Phalanx CIWS (3 on *Nimitz* and *Eisenhower*).

Aircraft: Up to 86 aircraft, 20 F-14, 18 F/A-18, 20 A-6E, 10 S-3A, 5 EA-6B, 5E-2C, 8 SH-3D.

Right: The sheer size of these nuclear carriers can be gauged by the way in which the aircraft are dwarfed on the flight-deck. The ship's own armament is relatively light.

Below: USS *Carl Vinson* (CVN 70) on sea trials, before arrival of her carrier air wing. Maximum width of the flight-deck, seen clearly here, is 293ft (89.4m).

The aircraft carrier is today's capital ship and, for a few years more, at least, remains the epitome of naval might. Since the middle of World War II the United States has always had the largest carrier fleet by a wide margin. The British carrier fleet gradually diminished over the years until today where there are only three light fleet carriers. These are capable of operating V/STOL Harriers and helicopters, but not ASW and EW fixed-wing aircraft. A few other countries such as Brazil and Argentina operate a single aircraft carrier, but only France and India have two. France is the only nation, other than the United States and the USSR, planning to build nuclear-powered aircraft carriers.

The expansion of Soviet naval power has led to the need for carriers. First came the Moskva class with a full-width flight-deck abaft the stack and a complement of 14 helicopters. Next to appear was the much larger (43,000 tons full load displacement) Kiev class, with an angled flight-deck and capable of operating both helicopters and V/STOL Forger aircraft. The next class, due to join the fleet in 1990, has a 65,000 ton displacement and is likely to operate conventional take-off and landing (CTOL) carrier-borne aircraft.

The original nuclear-powered carrier was USS *Enterprise* (CVN 65) (92,200 tons full load displacement), which was built in the remarkably short time of three years nine months and commissioned in 1961. She was so successful that, when the time came to plan a replacement for the Midway class, nuclear power was the preferred means of propulsion. Technological advances meant that *Enterprise*'s eight 35,000shp A2W reactors could be replaced by just two 130,000shp A4W reactors. In addition, the uranium cores need to be replaced much less frequently.

The reduction in the number of reactors has also permitted major improvements to be made in the internal arrangements below hangar deck level. In *Enterprise* the entire centre section of the ship is occupied by machinery rooms with the aviation fuel compartments and the missile magazines pushed out towards the ends of the ship, but in *Nimitz* the propulsion machinery is divided into two separate units with the magazines between and forward of them. The improved layout has resulted in an increase of 20 per cent in aviation fuel capacity and a similar increase in the volume available for munitions and stores. The flight-deck layout for the Nimitz class is almost identical to that of the *John F Kennedy* (CV 67).

Class History

The Nimitz class aircraft carriers are the mightiest and most powerful warships in history. Each ship normally carries some 90 aircraft with capabilities ranging from nuclear strike, through interception and ground-attack to close-in anti-submarine protection. This represents a more powerful and better balanced tactical air wing than is possessed by many nations in their entire air force.

Built as replacements for the Midway class (67,500 tons full load displacement), the *Nimitz* class was the subject of considerable political controversy in its early days. *Nimitz* (CVN 68) was authorised in Fiscal Year 1967, but *Eisenhower* and *Vinson* were not authorised until Fiscal Year 1970 and Fiscal Year 1974 respectively.

Each carrier is manned by a crew of 3,300 men with an air wing of a further 3,000 men. Their nuclear reactors have cores which enable them to operate for 13 years at a stretch, equivalent to steaming some 1 million miles. Such extraordinary statistics will only be challenged when the Soviet Navy's nuclear-powered super-carriers enter service in the 1990s, and it is, in fact, to counter the perceived threat from these United States carriers that has caused such massive developments in the Soviet Navy over the past 15 years. Delays in construction caused by shipyard problems resulted in rocketing costs and, in the late-1970s, the Carter Administration attempted unsuccessfully in Congress to block authorisation funds for the construction of a fourth carrier in favour of a smaller (50,000 ton), conventionally-powered design, known as the "CVV". However, the Reagan Administration committed itself to the continuation of the CVN progamme, with at least two further ships beyond the *George Washington* (CVN 73) being projected.

The current deployment is that *Roosevelt* and *Eisenhower* both serve in the Atlantic, while *Vinson* and *Nimitz* are in the Pacific.

Above: The Nimitz class carriers of the US Navy are the mightiest and most powerful ships of war ever built. They carry an air wing of some 90 aircraft together with great amounts of weaponry and fuel.

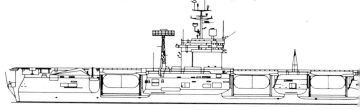

Armament

The provision of defensive weapons and sensors on the first two of the class, *Nimitz* (CVN 68) and *Eisenhower* (CVN 69) was initially on a par with that on the conventionally-powered *Kennedy* (CV 67). However, the third ship, *Vinson* (CVN 70), has NATO Sea Sparrow and Phalanx in place of the BPDMS launchers on earlier ships, and these have since been fitted to the earlier ships. This parallels the increase in defensive armament taking place on the carriers of other navies. All are also fitted with a very sophisticated and comprehensive ASW classification and analysis centre (ASCAC) which permits instant sharing of target data between the carrier, its ASW aircraft and escorting ships. The ASCAC also has direct satellite links into other ASW centres, e.g. at SACLANT in Norfolk, Virginia, which enables it to play a very significant role in the overall ASW battle at both strategic and tactical levels.

The armament of the carriers makes an interesting comparison with that of the Soviet carriers. The American super-carriers mount just four Phalanx 20mm CIWS (three on CVN 68/69) and three Mark 29 launchers for NATO Sea Sparrow (four on CVN 70). The latest Soviet Kiev class carrier, *Baku*, has an armament of 12 SS-N-12, two SA-N-3 SAM launchers, a so-far unknown number of SA-N-9 SAM launchers, two single 100mm DP guns and eight 30mm Gatling CIWS.

Aircraft

The true power of the Nimitz class CVNs lies, however, in their air wing, which is of exceptional strength. Airborne early warning (AEW) is provided by five Grumman E-2C Hawkeye and electronic defence by five Grumman EA-6B Prowler aircraft. Attack capability centres on 18 McDonnell Douglas F/A-18 Hornets and 20 Grumman A-6E Intruder, with four Grumman KA-6D air-to-air refuelling aircraft in support. Air defence is provided by 20 Grumman F-14A Tomcat. ASW aircraft include ten Lockheed S-3A Viking fixed-wing and eight Sikorsky SH-3H Sea King helicopters.

Protection

Until 1945 all battleships incorporated very considerable armoured protection, while aircraft carriers had almost no armour, although some British carriers had an armoured flight-deck. Thereafter little or no armoured protection was included until the Nimitz class, which has flight-decks and hulls constructed of high-tensile steel, which is intended to limit the effect of semi-armour-piercing bombs. In addition, the "Improved" Nimitz class have been built with Kevlar armour over "vital spaces" and this will be added to the older Nimitz class carriers during refits.

Future

Two carriers of this class — *Abraham Lincoln* (CVN 72) and *George Washington* (CVN 73) — are being commissioned in 1989 and 1991 respectively. When the last of these (CVN 73) is commissioned USS *Coral Sea* (CV 43), a Midway class carrier commissioned in 1947, will be retired from the front-line force to become a training carrier. Two further carriers are planned; of these CVN 74 is due to join the fleet in 1996 and CVN 75 in 1997.

All Nimitz class carriers will undergo the normal refits, but they will start entering their 28-month service life extension programme (SLEP) periods in 2004. Currently projected SLEPs are: *Nimitz* 2004-2006, *Eisenhower* 2007-2009, *Vinson* 2010-2012 and *Roosevelt* 2014-2016.

Below: Nimitz class in side elevation showing the great length of 1,092ft (332.9m), and the three side elevators, which can move aircraft between flight-deck and hangar without interrupting flying operations. The single, compact, neatly-designed superstructure also leaves the large flight-deck clear and uncluttered.

Iowa Class

Origin: United States.
Displacement: 45,000 tons standard; 58,000 tons full load.
Dimensions: Length overall 887.2ft (270.4m); beam 108.2ft (33m); draught 38ft (11.6m). (*New Jersey* length 887.6ft (270.5m).
Propulsion: 4 geared turbines; 212,000shp; 4 shafts.
Performance: 35 knots; 5,000nm at 30 knots, 14,800 nm at 20 knots.
Built: 1940 to 1944.
Ships: *Iowa* (BB-61), *New Jersey* (BB-62), *Missouri* (BB-63), *Wisconsin* (BB-64).

Above: USS *New Jersey*. On the foredeck are two of the three 16in (406mm) turrets, each weighing 1,700 tons and needing a crew of 77 men.

Complement: 1,520 (65 officers, 1,415 ratings, 2 marine officers, 38 marines).
Armament: SSM: 4 octuple box launchers for Tomahawk (32) and 4 quad launchers for Harpoon (16). Guns: 3 triple 16in (406mm)/50 (9); 6 twin 5in (127mm)/38 (12) and 4 20mm Mark 15 Phalanx CIWS.
Aircraft: Four LAMPS II/III helicopters.

In its day the battleship was incontestably the most powerful warship afloat and was the symbol by which naval power was measured. All major, and some minor, navies entered World War II with battleships in their inventory, but in the space of just three years (1942 to 1945) they were displaced into second importance by aircraft carriers. All but a very few battleships had been put into reserve by 1950 and after a further ten years or so they were all scrapped, with the sole exception of the US Navy's Iowa class. Other battleships, such as the German *Bismarck* and *Tirpitz,* and the Japanese *Yamato* seem to have disappeared from the naval scene long, long ago; the US Navy's Iowa class were not only built at the same time but they have also just begun a totally new period of front-line service, which looks likely to last well into the twenty-first century.

Class History

Design work on the Iowa class started in 1936. The new class was to be armed with nine 16in (406mm)/50 guns in three three-gun turrets and 20 5in (127mm)/38 dual-purpose guns. Also, very powerful (212,000shp) engines would make them the fastest battleships ever built. In addition, they were to be very well armoured with a 12.1in (30.7cm) main belt, designed to survive direct engagement with enemy ships armed with 18in (460mm) guns (i.e. the Japanese Yamato class which were then being built, in great secrecy, for the Imperial Japanese Navy).

Six ships were laid down, of which four were commissioned: *Iowa*, February 22, 1943; *New Jersey*, May 23, 1943; *Missouri*, June 11, 1944; *Wisconsin*, April 16, 1944. They all fought with great distinction in the Pacific campaign, with the Japanese surrender being signed aboard the USS *Missouri* in Tokyo Bay on September 2, 1945. The last two ships of the class, the *Illinois* (BB 65) and the *Kentucky* (BB 66), were not completed; the former was cancelled in 1945 and the latter was eventually launched in 1950, but no further work was done and it was sold for scrap in 1958.

Three of the four ships which had fought in the war were decommissioned in the late-1940s, although the *Missouri* remained in commission. All four rejoined the active list during the Korean War (1950-53) and were used in the

Below: The return to service of these ships is a great success story with their unique combination of heavy armament, speed, endurance and armoured protection.

shore bombardment role. All were decommissioned in the mid late-1950s, but the *New Jersey* was reactivated in April 1968 for the Vietnam War only to be decommissioned for the third time in December 1969.

Following the appearance of the Soviet Navy's Kirov class battlecruisers it was decided to reactivate the Iowas to provide, in the words of, the then, Secretary of Defense, Caspar Weinberger, "a valuable supplement to the carrier force in performing presence and strike missions, while substantially increasing our ability to provide naval gunfire support for power projection and amphibious assault missions."

On December 28, 1982 the *New Jersey* joined the Pacific Fleet and started her first operational deployment on June 9, 1983, serving first in Central American waters and later off Lebanon, to return to the United States on May 5, 1984. this is reckoned to have been the longest US Navy peacetime deployment, with 322 days at sea, covering a distance of some 76,000 miles (122,307km). The *Iowa* was recommissioned on April 28, 1984 and was followed by the *Missouri* (July 1986) and the *Wisconsin* (January 1988).

The reactivation programme has involved the modernisation of all electronic and communications equipment, renovation of all accommodation and domestic utilities to meet contemporary standards, conversion to US Navy distillate fuel, reshaping the afterdeck to provide landing facilities (but no hangars) for four LAMPS helicopters and the removal of extraneous equipment (e.g. the aircraft crane). It was planned at one time to remove the rear turret to make room for a proper aircraft hangar; this idea has, however, been dropped.

Armament

Main armament is nine massive 16in (406mm) guns firing armour-piercing projectiles weighing up to 2,700lb (1,225kg). These have a maximum range of 23 miles (39km) at a theoretical rate of two rounds per gun per minute. There is, quite simply, no similar weapon on any other warship in any navy. These guns can be used for both anti-ship missions or in the shore bombardment role. Both barrels and ammunition are long out of production, but no fewer than 34 spare barrels remain in storage, together with over 20,000 shells.

The secondary armament comprises 5in (127mm) guns, but four of the original 20 turrets have been removed to make way for four 8-missile Mark 143 Tomahawk SLCM launchers. Also, four quadruple Harpoon SSM launchers have been fitted each side of the after funnel and four Phalanx CIWS mounts are fitted: two just forward of the foremost funnel and two forward of the after funnel.

Below: Long-range firepower is provided by the Tomahawk cruise missile, here seen on a test launch from USS *New Jersey*. The Iowas can carry 32 of these, either in the anti-ship role in a land attack version using a nuclear, conventional or multi-munition warhead.

Protection

The protection built-in to these battleships represents the requirements of a bygone era, being designed to resist 18in (460mm) shells. Modern warships are built to totally different standards, with virtually no armoured protection, which, as was shown by the British losses in the Falklands War, leaves them very vulnerable. The Iowa class, however, is effectively invulnerable to sea-skimming missiles with hollow-charge warheads, such as the French Exocet and Soviet ASMs, while no other surface warship remains with a gun which could compete with the Iowas' 16in (406mm) main armament.

The hull has a triple bottom for most of its length with four rows of longitudinal bulkheads forming three sets of tanks used for water and fuel. The main armoured belt is 500ft (152m) long, 20ft (6m) high and 9in (22cm) thick. It is angled inwards at 19 degrees to increase the effective thickness presented to an incoming shell. The estimated effectiveness of the armour is that it would stop one of Iowa's own 16in (406mm) shells at a range of 10.25nm (19km). Horizontal protection is provided by three armoured decks, 1.5in (38mm), 1.25in (32mm) and 0.5in (13mm) thick, respectively.

The three 16in (406mm) gun turrets are heavily armoured, with 17in (432mm) fronts, 7.2in (184mm) roofs and 12in (305mm) backs. The superstructure housing the bridge and other command centres has vertical protection of 17.5in (444mm), horizontal protection of 4in (102mm) and overhead protection of 7.2in (184mm). In addition, all critical electric and electronic cables run through armoured conduits. It would appear that the only ways in which the Iowas could be critically damaged in modern warfare would be by aircraft bombs, several heavy torpedoes or a nuclear weapon.

No air defence missile systems are carried and the only ASW weapons systems are four LAMPS-II/III helicopters and Nixie torpedo decoys. It is the mission of the task group in company with the Iowas to prevent enemy aircraft and submarines from reaching a position from which they can deliver their weapons.

Sensors

Sensors are among the most expensive items of modern equipment and, to keep costs down, the Iowas have not been fitted with as many systems as they might have been. The ships have kept the gunfire control systems, but have been fitted with up-to-date communications systems; e.g. for satellite systems. All four ships are to have drones for target spotting for the main battery.

Conclusion

The reactivation of these ships was a triumph achieved at a cost for each ship of less than that for a new frigate of the Oliver Hazard Perry class. The US Navy owes a large debt of gratitude to the man who decided to preserve these fine ships instead of scrapping them, as was done in every other navy. Indeed, the Royal Navy could well regret the passing of HMS *Vanguard,* the finest British battleship, completed in 1946 and scrapped in 1960. Similarly, the French who broke up the splendid *Richelieu* and *Jean Bart,* in 1964 and 1970 respectively. All three, had they still been in existence today, could have been given equally cost- and combat-effective rejuvenations and could have provided the same combination of firepower and combat persistence as the Iowas today.

Below: The Iowa class, as reactivated in the 1980s. Four LAMPS II/III helicopters are carried, but there are no hangar facilities. Plans for a flight-deck for V/STOL aircraft (e.g. AV-8B) have been dropped.

Kirov Class

Origin: USSR.
Displacement: 24,000 tons standard; 28,000 tons full load.
Dimensions: Length overall 814ft (248m); beam 92ft (28m); draught 29ft (8.8m).
Propulsion: CONAS; 2 nuclear reactors plus two oil-fired boilers, steam turbines; 150,000shp; 2 shafts.
Performance: 33 kots; 3,000nm at 33 knots (CONAS), 150,000nm at 25 knots (nuclear only).
Built: 1977 to 1989.
Ships: *Kirov, Frunze, Kalinin* in service; one more due in service 1992.
Complement: 800 (approximate).
Armament: Missile launchers: 20 SS-N-19 (20 missiles); 12 SA-N-6 (96); 2 twin SA-N-4 (40); (*Frunze* only) 16 SA-N-9 (128). Guns: 2 single 100mm (*Kirov*); 1 twin 130mm (*Frunze*); 8 30mm CIWS. ASW weapons: 1 twin SS-N-14 (*Kirov* only); 1 RBU-6000; 2 RBU-1000. Torpedo tubes: 2 quintuple 21in (533mm).
Aircraft: 3 Kamov Ka-25 Hormone or Ka-37 Helix ASW helicopters.

Right: These are, in fact, the largest surface warships, apart from aircraft carriers, to be built since World War II. They also show the extraordinary ability of Soviet ship designers to be innovative, perhaps because they are uncluttered with the traditions which beset Western designers. Thus they carry vertical launch systems for their missiles and are powered by a totally new combined nuclear and steam (CONAS) system.

Recent Soviet naval construction has shown a consistent trend towards larger ships with greater firepower, longer range and increased endurance for distant-water operations. The latest example is the Kirov class, the largest surface combatants, other than aircraft carriers, to be built by any navy since the end of World War II. Their size, heavy armament and general sophistication have impressed Western navies, and their appearance resulted in the US Navy refurbishing the four Iowa class battleships. The Kirov class battlecruiser appears to have two major roles: first, to be the lynchpin of the escort for aircraft carriers in high threat areas and, secondly, as a flagship for an independent surface action task force.

Class History

Classified by the Soviet Navy as "atomny raketny kreyser" (nuclear-powered missile cruisers) the Kirov class is a descendant of the battle-cruiser, a controversial concept which originated with the Royal Navy in the 1900s for large, heavily-armed and fast capital ships, which achieved their high speed at the expense of very light armoured protection.

Three of these Soviet ships, *Kirov*, *Frunze* and *Kalinin* are now at sea. There are several important differences between the first two, stemming from a switch in emphasis in armament, although both are exceptionally well-armed; the third ship has yet to be sighted by Western observers and may well have still further changes in weapons and sensors. The *Kirov* weapon and sensor fit shows a tendency towards ASW, whereas the *Frunze* shows more of a tendency towards the air-defence role. The differences may, however, simply be part of testing the operational capabilities of various armament fits.

Above: A stern view of a Kirov class battlecruiser, showing her flight-deck and the large door for the variable-depth sonar (VDS) system. Three helicopters are carried, either Hormone A or B, or Helix. They are provided with a very spacious flight-deck and enter their hangar through a ramp covered by a sliding door at its forward end. The gun turrets are mounted above the flight-deck: two single 100mm in *Kirov* and a twin 130mm in *Frunze*.

Armament

In place of the big guns of earlier capital ships the Kirov class has a powerful battery of 20 long-range SS-N-19 surface-to-surface missile launchers, housed in a multi-cell vertical-launch battery (probably armoured) located in the forecastle. Over-the-horizon (OTH) targetting data for these 300nm (555km) range missiles is supplied either by a command post ashore via a communications satellite link, or direct by surveillance satellites using electronic intelligence, active radar, infra-red detection techniques, or by the on-board helicopters.

Both *Kirov* and *Frunze* have sophisticated air defence systems. The SA-N-6 SAM is a new high-performance system, using a track-via-missile (TVM) guidance system, which enables the ship to keep a number of missiles in the air simultaneously, thus engaging multiple targets. The missile itself has a range in excess of 46.5nm (80km) and a speed of Mach 5 to 6. The 12 launchers are even supplied by a rotating eight-round magazine.

In *Kirov* the only short-range air-defence missile system is SA-N-4, a "pop-up" launcher housed in a magazine bin containing 18 to 20 missiles, but in *Frunze* these are supplemented by SA-N-9. Also, in *Kirov* all air-defence missile launchers are on the forecastle, which leaves the after quadrant somewhat naked. This has been rectified in *Frunze* by siting two 4-tube SA-N-8 launchers on the quarter-deck, displacing the 30mm Gatling CIWS which have been moved to the after superstructure.

Kirov mounts two single, dual-purpose 3.9in (100mm) guns aft, but in *Frunze* these have been replaced by a single twin 5.1in (130mm) turret, identical to those fitted to the Sovremenny and Slava classes. Close-range anti-missile defence in both ships comprises four groups of two 30mm Gatling guns, sited in the four "corners" of the ship to give all-round coverage.

These Soviet ships are designed to play a major part in their own anti-submarine defence, although there would, of course, be an escort of destroyers or frigates. *Kirov* has a reloadable launcher for SS-N-14 ASW missiles on the forecastle (deleted on *Frunze*), and both ships have RBU-type ASW rocket launchers, torpedo tubes and three Kamov Ka-25 Hormone-A/B (or Ka-32 Helix) helicopters for ASW and missile guidance.

Protection

Unlike the US Navy's Iowa class battleships, the Soviet Kirov class battlecruisers do not appear to incorporate any armoured protection. Evidence of such an assertion is provided by the rows of portholes in the hull. There may, however, be some armouring of particular areas, such as the combat information centre. The Kirovs are thus likely to be as vulnerable as any other modern warship to damage by anti-ship missiles and bombs, and would certainly have no protection at all against the 16in (406mm) guns of the Iowa class battleships.

Sensors

There is a large low-frequency (LF) sonar in the bow and an LF variable-depth sonar (VDS) in the stern. The extensive electronics suite includes two major

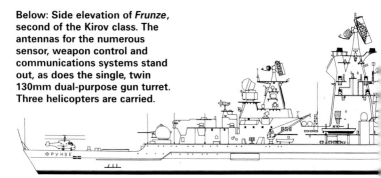

Below: Side elevation of *Frunze*, second of the Kirov class. The antennas for the numerous sensor, weapon control and communications systems stand out, as does the single, twin 130mm dual-purpose gun turret. Three helicopters are carried.

3-D air surveillance radars, "Top Pair" and "Top Steer", plus individual gun and missile fire control radars. *Kirov* is fitted with the standard 1970s ECM/ESM outfit, with eight Side Globe broad-band jammers and four Rum Tub ESM antennas around the top of the tower mast. Neither of these are fitted in *Frunze*, each being replaced by a different type of bell-shaped radome. The communications fit is also changed in the newer ship, the main visible change being the replacement of *Kirov*'s Vee-Tube C by large, bell-covered satellite antennas. This appears to represent a logical change in emphasis from long distance HF communications, notoriously liable to interception and jamming, to satellite links which are both more secure and able to handle much greater traffic volumes.

Conclusion

Kalinin entered service in 1989 and it is known that at least one more Kirov class ship is under construction. Both will certainly include yet further refinements of the weapons systems, while their sensor fits may well also incorporate the new phased-array radars, which were seen for the first time in the West when *Baku*, the fourth Kiev class aircraft carrier sailed through the Bosphorous on June 8, 1988.

There is no further information on the Soviet Navy's plans beyond that, although, having discovered the value of such large ships in peacetime power projection, to say nothing of their value in war, it can safely be assumed that further, and perhaps even larger classes, will be built.

Above: This photograph, taken from a Royal Navy Lynx helicopter, shows to advantage the long, sleek forecastle of the *Frunze* which conceals vertical launch systems for SA-N-9, SA-N-6 and SS-N-19 missiles. Note also the RBU-6000 ASW rocket launcher.

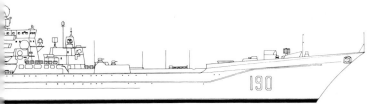

Slava Class

All ships of this class are fitted out as flagships.

Origin: USSR.
Displacement: 10,000 tons standard; 12,500 tons full load.
Dimensions: Length overall 607.9ft (185.3m); beam 65.6ft (20.0m); draught 21ft (6.4m).
Propulsion: COGOG; 4 boost gas-turbines, 30,000hp each; 2 cruise gas-turbines, 12,000hp each; 2 propellers, 120,000hp 33 knots.
Performance: 2,000nm at 30 knots, 8,800nm at 15 knots.
Built: 1976 to 1983.
Ships: *Slava, Marshal Ustinov,* (+2).
Complement: 720.
Armament: SSM: 16 SS-N-12 launchers (16 missiles). SAM: 8 SA-N-6 vertical launchers (64 missiles). 2 twin SA-N-4 launchers (40 missiles). Guns: 1 twin 130mm, 70 cal. DP. 6 ADMG 30mm CIWS. ASW: 2 12-barrelled RBU-6000. 2 quintuple 21in (533mm) M-57 torpedo tubes.
Aircraft: 1 Kamov Ka-25 Hormone-B or Kamov Ka-27 Helix ASW helicopter.

Up to the end of World War II cruisers were the second largest type of gun-armed surface warship after battleships. Their guns ranged from 6in (152mm) to 8in (203mm) in calibre and usually had a belt of armour, although obviously not as effective as that of a battleship. Their displacement ranged from 6,000 to 12,000 tons. Originally envisaged as either commerce raiders or for the protection of trade routes, their mission eventually evolved into acting as outer screens to battleship or aircraft carrier task groups, although sometimes the cruisers formed light, fast task groups of their own.

After the war battleships disappeared very rapidly, but cruisers remained as the heaviest type of escort vessel for aircraft carriers, especially for protection against aircraft and surface ships. Cruisers also were of sufficient size to provide platforms for missile systems and their associated sensors.

Below: The large launch-bins for SS-N-12 anti-ship missiles are unique to this design. Re-loading at sea is not possible.

Class History

The first class of Soviet post-war cruisers were the Sverdlovs (17,200 tons), armed with 12 6in (152mm) guns. These were intended to attack NATO convoys and naval units in the Atlantic, somewhat in the manner of German "pocket battleships" such as *Scharnhorst, Gneisenau* and *Graf Spee* in World War II. The Sverdlovs were followed by rather smaller cruisers, with two distinct roles. The first type were anti-submarine cruisers ("Bol'shoy Protivolodochnyy Korabl"), of which the Kresta II class (7,700 tons) and Kara class (9,700 tons) both appeared in 1969. The second type were missile cruisers with a primary anti-surface role. First of these was the Kynda class (5,700 tons) of the 1960s, followed a few years later by the Kresta I class (7,500 tons).

Then came the Slava class, initially known in the West as BLACKCOM 1 (BLACK Sea COMbattant), as it was being built at the Nikolayev North shipyard on the Black Sea. Then, for a short period it was designated the Krasina class,

Left: With a displacement of 12,500 tons and a length of 608ft (185m) the Slava class are among the largest warships at sea.

Below: *Slava* at sea, with a Kamov Ka-25 Hormone-B helicopter on the stern flight-deck. The aircraft is needed to provide mid-course guidance for the SS-N-12 anti-ship missiles.

79

before the first ship was finally observed at sea and the correct Soviet name *Slava* ("Glory") discovered. Since then a further two ships have been launched at least one more is under construction.

Armament
There had been some surprise in the West when the Kresta II class appeared in the 1960s, with its fixed battery of eight launchers mounted alongside the bridge and it was remarked that the Soviet designers were putting all the ship's armament "in the shop window". There was even greater surprise, however, when the *Slava* revealed its unique battery of SS-N-12 SSMs in fixed launch tubes sited *"en echelon"* along either side of the bridge superstructure. The object of this design is presumably to provide the ship with as large a number of missiles as possible, whilst avoiding the complexity and expense of automatic reloading devices.

The main armament comprises 16 SS-N-12 SSMs in two rows of four twin launchers mounted at a fixed elevation of about 8 degrees. These are located either side of the forward superstructure; there are no reloads. The only other anti-ship weapon is the twin 5in (130mm) automatic gun.

Anti-aircraft weapons consist of two rows of four SA-N-6 SAM silos between the funnels and the aircraft hangar, with a twin SA-N-4 silo at each side of the after end of the hangar. Finally, there is the usual Soviet close-in system comprising six 30mm Gatlings, two on the forward superstructure and four (two each side) just forward of the funnel.

ASW weapons comprise quintuple fixed 21in (533mm) torpedo tubes either side of the aircraft hangar and two RBU-6000 forward of the bridge. There is also a Hormone-B or Helix ASW helicopter, with a and hangar at the stern.

Sensors
Surveillance 3D: One Top Pair.
One Top Steer.
Fire Control: One Front Door/Front Piece (SS-N-12).
One Top Dome (SA-N-6).
Two Pop Group (SA-N-4).
Three Bass Tilt (30mm Gatlings).
One Kite Screech (130mm).
EW: Eight Side Globe. Four Rum Tub.
Electro-optical: Two Tee Plinth.
Navigation: Three Palm Frond.
Bow-mounted Sonar: One MF/LF.
Stern-mounted VDS: One MF.

Below: *Slava* in the Mediterreanean. The pennant number differs from that shown on pages 78-79, as the Soviets allocate such numbers for tactical purposes; when the mission changes so does the number.

Future

These large ships have nothing revolutionary in their design and even the hull lines are of a very simple, almost "slabsided" configuration. The armament, too, is straightforward, using existing weapons and sensors. In fact, it is generally agreed that they were constructed against the possible failure of the even larger but far more adventurous Kirov designs. Nevertheless, the Slavas are very powerful units, clearly intended for major actions against surface fleets, and an armament of 16 SS-N-12s gives a very respectable over-the-horizon capability. They also possess very useful air defence and ASW capabilities, with a full range of sensors and a comprehensive selection of weapons. They are clearly capable of distant-water deployments, almost certainly as the flagship of a surface-action task group.

Above: This superb overhead shot of a Slava class cruiser, shows her armament, and, in particular, the eight SA-N-6 launchers abaft the stacks.

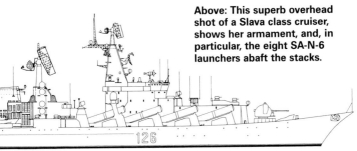

Above: *Slava* in profile, showing her large bridge and spacious superstructure, the whole dominated by the huge Top Pair antenna. Note also the crane, with its jib resting between the twin stacks.

C70 Class (ASW and AA).

Origin:	France.
Displacement:	C70 (ASW) — 3,830 tons standard; 4,170 tons full load. C70 (AA) — 3,820 tons standard; 4,340 tons full load.
Dimensions:	Length overall 455.9ft (139m); beam 45.9ft (14m); draught 18.04ft (5.5m).
Propulsion:	C70 (ASW) — CODOG. 2 Rolls-Royce Olympus TM3B gas-turbines, 2 SEMT-Pielstick 16 PA 6 CV 280 diesels; 2 shafts; 52,000hp (gas-turbine), 10,400hp (diesel). C70 (AA) — 4 SEMT-Pielstick 18PA6 BTC "diesels rapides"; 2 shafts; 42,300hp.
Performance:	C70 ASW — 30 knots (gas-turbine), 21 knots (diesel); 1,000nm at 30 knots, 9,500nm at 17 knots (diesel). C70 AA — 29.6 knots; 4,800nm at 24 knots, 8,200nm at 17 knots.
Built:	C70 (ASW) — 1974 to 1990. C70 (AA) — 1982 to 1990.
Ships:	C70 (ASW) — *Georges Leygues* (D 640); *Dupleix* (D 641); *Montcalm* (D 642); *Jean de Vienne* (D 643); *Primauguet* (D 644); *La Motte-Picquet* (D 645); *Latouche-Treville* (D 646). C70 (AA) — *Cassard* (D 614); *Jean Bart* (D 615).
Complement:	C70 (ASW) — 18 officers, 210 ratings. C70 (AA) — 12 officers, 229 ratings.
Armament:	C70 (ASW) — 8 Exocet SSM (4 in *Georges Leygues* and *Dupleix*), 1 Crotale SAM launcher (8 plus 18 reloads), 1 100mm DP gun, 2 L5 ASW torpedo catapults (10), 2 20mm AA guns. C70 (AA) — 1 Mark 13 launcher (20 Standard SAM), 8 Exocet SSM, 1 100mm DP gun, 2 SADRAL point-defence SAM (12 missiles), 2 L5 ASW torpedo catapults (10), 2 20mm AA guns.
Aircraft:	C70 (ASW) — 2 Lynx ASW helicopters. C70 (AA) — 1 light helicopter.

Left: *Georges Leygues* at sea. The basic hull is used for seven ASW and two AA vessels with appropriate weapons/sensor fits.

Most navies possess warships in the 3,000 to 6,000 ton bracket, some of which are designated destroyers and others frigates. In World War II destroyers were larger than frigates, but the general rule today is that those specialising in the ASW mission are frigates, the others destroyers. Within the category of destroyers, there are generally two mission specialisations: anti-surface and anti-aircraft.

Above: Since World War II, the French Navy has produced a very successful line of destroyers, culminating in the very efficient C70 ASW and AA classes.

Left: The fine lines of *Montcalm* (D 642) are dominated by the large funnel. The bridge has proved to be too low in bad weather and is being raised by one deck level in the last three of the class.

The latter anti-aircraft mission has become extremely important, especially in defending high-value units, such as aircraft carriers and battleships, against attacking aircraft and missiles. The French Navy will base its future operations on two task groups centred on the two carriers, currently *Clemenceau* (R 98) and *Foch* (R 99), and in future the nuclear-powered *Charles de Gaulle* (R 91) and a second unit as yet un-named. These carrier battle groups (CVBG) will require the full range of anti-air, anti-submarine and surface warfare capabilities from their escorts. The principle escorts for the French carriers will be the destroyers of the C70 (ASW) and C70 (AA) classes.

Class History

The French Navy has a long tradition of large, well-designed, powerful and very capable destroyers, the latest in this long line being the C70 class. In this design the same hull has been used to accommodate two very different warship types: the seven-ship Georges Leygues C70 (ASW) class and the two-ship Cassard C70 (AA) class.

Developed from the *Tourville* (F 67), name ship of its class, the original C70s are the ASW Georges Leygues class, which the French Navy originally classified as "corvettes". All seven are now in service, an eighth having been cancelled as an economy measure. There are two versions of the C70 (ASW), the fifth and subsequent ships being fitted with a towed array in place of the DUBV-43B variable depth sonar, the new Crotale Navale EDIR SAM system, a new 100mm compact gun and the Vampir Infra-Red Surveillance system. These ships also have the bridge built one deck level higher to overcome the problems experienced by the first four in bad weather. Of these modifications only the Crotale Navale SAM system is likely to be retrofitted into the first four of the class.

The anti-aircraft version of the C70, the Cassard class, is designed to provide the anti-aircraft and anti-missile defences for an aircraft-carrier task group or a mercantile convoy. These ships have a very different armament and propulsion system to the C70 (ASW), but are installed in an identical hull.

Propulsion differs between the two types. The Georges Leygues ships are powered by a CODOG system, comprising two Olympus gas-turbines and two SEMT-Pielstick diesels, whilst propulsion for the Cassard class is provided by four SEMT-Pielstick 18PA6 low-compression diesels. It is claimed that these provide a system which is virtually as light and easy-to-maintain as gas-turbines, but without the need for large air intakes and exhaust trunking. This is particularly important in the Cassard design, in which a lot of aluminium alloy has had to be used in the superstructure to save top weight. This is a step which the French designers may now be regretting in view of recent naval experiences with aluminium alloys in warships.

Armament

In the Georges Leygues class the principle ASW systems are L5 ASW torpedoes and two Westland Lynx helicopters. Main surface weapons are eight MM40 Exocet SSMs (four MM-38 in *Georges Leygues* and *Dupleix*) and one 100mm DP Model 1968 gun mounted on the forecastle. Air defence is provided by an 8-cell Crotale missile launcher mounted on the hangar roof.

On the C70 (AA) class, the main AA armament is one single-arm Mark 13 launcher mounted aft for 40 Standard SM-1 (MR) SAM missiles, supplemented by the SADRAL short-range self-defence missile system and a single, forecastle-mounted, dual-purpose Creusot-Loire 100mm/55 (3.9in) gun. Surface warfare weapons systems include eight MM-40 Exocets, plus, of course, the 100mm gun. Sonar is fitted and there are two hull-mounted quintuple ASW torpedo launchers. Only one light helicopter is carried.

Sensors

All vessels of both types use Decca navigation radars: C70 (ASW) have the Decca RM 1226 (French designation DRBN 32) and C70 (AA) the Decca 1229. Air search is the French DRBV 26 in the first four and DRBV 15A in the final three C70 (ASW), while the C70 (AA) has the DRBV 26 together with the much more sophisticated DRBJ 11B.

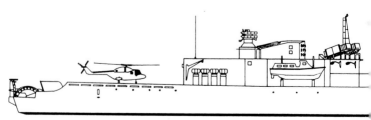

Fire control for the 100mm gun was initially provided by DRBC 32D, but all ships will soon have the frequency agile, monopulse DRBC 33, with a CSEE Panda optronic backup director. C70 (AA) also have the American-designed SPG-51C tracking radar for the Standard SM-1 MR SAM systems.

The last three C70 (ASW) are fitted with DUBV 24C hull-mounted, LF (5 kHz) sonar, DUBV 43B, LF, variable depth sonar (VDS), and DSBV 61 towed, passive, VLF, linear arrays. It is intended that the first four ships of the class will have their earlier model sonar suites upgraded to this standard. C70 (AA) currently have the newer, but less sophisticated DUBA 25A sonar, but may also be fitted with the DSBV 61 towed array in the future.

All ships have comprehensive EW suites and are also fitted with chaff/IR deception rocket launchers. C70 (ASW) have two short-range Dagaie RL, while the C70 (AA) have two Dagaie and two of the longer range Sagaie RL.

All ships are fitted with SENIT combat information systems. C70 (ASW) have the French-designed SENIT 4, which is built around the Iris N 55 computer. C70 (AA) have the later SENIT 6, which uses a number of M 15 computers together with the latest generation of display devices. Both systems integrate manual and automatic information inputs to establish the combat situation, and disseminate data automatically to other ships using Links 11 or 14. They also assist in decision-making and disseminate target-designation information.

Conclusion

These ships will provide the French Navy with a strong force of ASW and AA units, with all serving well into the next century. (They are scheduled to reach the end of their operational lives in 2013 and 2015.)

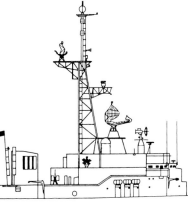

Above: A fine view of *Jean de Vienne* (D 643). These ships are fitted with comprehensive sensors and electronics equipment, controlled by the SENIT combat information system.

Below: Side profile of *Georges Leygues* (D 640). Clearly shown are the quad launchers for MM-38 Exocet abaft the stack.

Broadsword Class

Origin: United Kingdom.

Displacement: Batch 1 — 3,500 tons standard; 4,400 tons full load.
Batch 2 — 4,250 tons standard; 4,850 tons full load.
Batch 3 — 4,380 tons standard; 5,250 tons full load.

Dimensions: Batch 1 — Length overall 430ft (131.2m); beam 48.5ft (14.8m); draught 19.9ft (6m).
Batch 2 — Length overall 486ft (148.1m) (*Beaver, Boxer* 475ft (145m); beam (all) 48.4ft (14.75m); draught (all) 19.7ft (6.0m).
Batch 3 — Length overall 486ft (148.1m); beam 48.5ft (14.8m); draught 21ft (6.4m).

Propulsion: Batch 1 and *Boxer, Beaver* (both Batch 2) — COGOG; 2 Rolls-Royce Olympus TM3B gas turbines, 50,000shp; 2 Rolls-Royce Tyne RM1C gas turbines, 9,700shp; 2 shafts.
Batch 2 — *Brave* — COGOG; 2 Rolls-Royce Spey SM1A, 37,540shp; 2 Rolls-Royce Tyne RM1C gas turbines, 9,700shp; 2 shafts.
Batch 3 (all) and *London, Sheffield, Coventry* (Batch 2) — COGAG; 2 Rolls-Royce Spey SM1A gas turbines, 37,540shp; 2 Rolls-Royce Tyne RM1C gas turbines, 9,750shp; 2 shafts.

Performance: Batch 1 — 30 knots maximum, 18 knots on Tynes; 4,500nm on Tynes.
Batch 2 (*Brave*) — 32 knots maximum, 18 knots on Tynes; approximately 7,000nm at 18 knots on Tynes.
Batch 3 (all) and *London, Sheffield, Coventry* (Batch 2) — 30 knots maximum, 18 knots on Tynes; approximately 7,000nm at 18 knots on Tynes.

Built: Batch 1 — 1975 to 1980; Batch 2 — 1979 to 1986; Batch 3 — 1983 to 1988.

Ships: Batch 1 (Broadsword class) — *Broadsword* (F 88); *Battleaxe* (F 89); *Brilliant* (F 90); *Brazen* (F 91).
Batch 2 (Boxer class) — *Boxer* (F 92); *Beaver* (F 93); *Brave* (F 94), *London* (F 95); *Sheffield* (F 96); *Coventry* (F 97).
Batch 3 (Cornwall class) — *Cornwall* (F 99); *Cumberland* (F 85); *Campbelltown* (F 86); *Chatham* (F 87).

Complement: Batch 1 — 18 officers, 205 ratings.
Batch 2 — 19 officers, 246 ratings.
Batch 3 — 20 officers, 266 ratings.

Armament: 4 Exocet SSM (8 Harpoon on Batch 3), 2 Sea Wolf SAM (12 missiles), 2 STWS.1 ASW torpedo launchers (6 torpedoes), 2 40mm AA gun (30mm on Batch 2), 2 20mm AA (Batch 1 only) 1 114mm DP gun and 1 30mm CIWS (both on Batch 3 only).

Aircraft: 2 Lynx helicopters (EH 101 on Batch 3).

Right: HMS *Beaver*(F 93) a Type 22 Batch 2 frigate. Batch 2 and 3 ships are 41ft (12.5m) longer than Batch 1 to accommodate new weapons and sensors, to improve seaworthiness and to include the lessons of the Falklands War. Batch 2 ships have four Exocet launchers on the foredeck; in Batch 3 these are moved abaft the bridge, and a 4.5in (114mm) gun added.

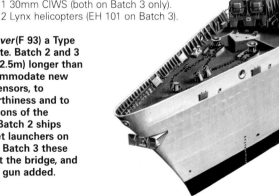

The term frigate has been used to describe various quite different types of warship over the past 200 years. However, it is now almost universally used to describe a small- to medium-sized warship whose primary mission is anti-submarine warfare. Thus, the Belgian Wielingen class (1,880 tons), the West German Bremen class (3,800 tons), the American Oliver Hazard Perry class (4,100 tons) and the British Type 23 Batch 3 class (5,250 tons) are all frigates. The latter are the largest ships in any navy to be designated "frigate".

Indeed, it is worth noting that, although still termed "frigates", the Type 22 Batch 3 ships are effectively multi-role destroyers, rather than ASW ships. In addition, the Batch 3s are virtually equal in dimensions and displacement to the Soviet Navy's Kynda class cruisers and larger than the British Type 42 design, which is classified as a destroyer!

Right: *Broadsword* **(F 88), a Type 22 Batch 1, at sea with one of her two Westland WG.13 Lynx helicopters parked on the spacious flight-deck.**

Class History

The British had an outstanding naval success with the Leander class of anti-submarine frigates, built in the early-1960s. The class has had an excellent record of service in the Royal Navy and has also sold well overseas. In looking for a successor the British first tried to agree a standard design with the Dutch, but this was unsuccessful and the British then went ahead on their own with the Type 22 design, while the Dutch developed the highly successful Kortenaer class.

The first of the new British class, HMS *Broadsword*, was commissioned on May 3, 1979, the remaining three of the first group, designated "Batch 1", being commissioned at yearly intervals thereafter. These ships are armed with two triple-torpedo tubes and carry two ASW helicopters, but they also have two Sea Wolf launchers, and an anti-ship capability in their two MM-39 Exocet missile launchers.

The Royal Navy decided to fit so many additional facilities that it became necessary to lengthen the hull by 41ft (12.49m), thus increasing displacement by some 600 tons. This group, designated Batch 2 (Boxer class), differ from Batch 1 principally in having enlarged action information organisation (AIO) facilities to handle data from the new Type 2031 towed array sonar. Two very useful by-products of stretching the basic Type 22 hull, however, are an increase in range (to nearly twice as much as Batch 1) and an increase in maximum speed of about 2 knots. In addition, water displacement fuel tanks have

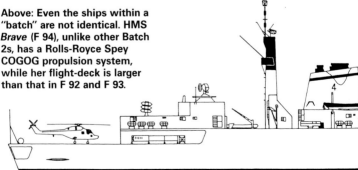

Above: Even the ships within a "batch" are not identical. HMS *Brave* (F 94), unlike other Batch 2s, has a Rolls-Royce Spey COGOG propulsion system, while her flight-deck is larger than that in F 92 and F 93.

been fitted to enable these ships to use virtually all their fuel (should this become necessary), without running into stability problems, although no captain would deliberately allow his fuel stocks to run so low, if it could be avoided. The first two ships of Batch 2 are otherwise identical to Batch 1 (i.e. propulsion, armament, etc.), but the remainder have different propulsion.

The final version (Batch 3) has the lengthened Batch 2 hull, but with much revised armament to incorporate the lessons of the 1982 Falklands War. This includes a Vickers 4.5in (115mm) gun on the foredeck, the replacement of Exocet SSMs by Harpoons, and the fitting of a Dutch-designed Goalkeeper CIWS.

Armaments

The Batch 1 ships have a primary ASW role and are armed with two triple STWS.1 ASW torpedo tubes and two Westland Lynx helicopters (normally one in peacetime). Principle air defence system is the Seawolf GWS.25, which proved so effective against both aircraft and anti-ship missiles in the 1982 Falklands War; there are two 6-missile launchers, one on the foredeck and the second on the hangar roof. There are also two single 40mm Bofors mounts, one each side of the foremast, and two 20mm Oerlikon GAM-B01 mounts, although these are not always installed. The only anti-ship weapons system is four MM-38 Exocet launchers, mounted in two pairs on the foredeck; there are no reloads.

Batch 2 ships have the same armament as Batch 1, but a larger flight-deck and hangar will enable them to embark the new EH-101 ASW helicopter when this enters service. It is also intended to replace the elderly 40mm Bofors with 30mm Rarden cannon in due course.

Batch 3 ships have significant armament changes from the previous two batches. Exocet is no longer carried and is replaced by the American-designed Harpoon system, with eight tubes mounted abaft the pilothouse, four firing to starboard and four to port. The deckspace released on the forecastle is used to mount a single 114mm Vickers Mark 8 dual-purpose gun, thus reversing the controversial "all-missile" armament policy of the earlier ships. Air defence system is the latest Sea Wolf GWS.25 Mod 3, supplemented by a single 30mm Goalkeeper and two 30mm Rarden LS-30B automatic cannon.

Conclusion

It is already planned to update the Batch 1 units by fitting newer weapons and sensors, wherever possible. This may include the replacement of Exocet by Harpoon and the fitting of the Type 2031 towed array in the Batch 1 ships. Sea Wolf GWS.25 Mod 3 will be fitted, although earlier plans to fit vertical launch tubes appear to have been abandoned.

The development of the Type 22 is of great interest as it shows how the influence of new equipment forces designers either to try and squeeze it into an existing hull or to lengthen the hull. A further factor in the Type 22 has been the Royal Navy's desire to incorporate the lessons learnt from actual combat during the 1982 Falklands War.

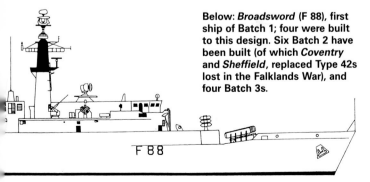

Below: *Broadsword* (F 88), first ship of Batch 1; four were built to this design. Six Batch 2 have been built (of which *Coventry* and *Sheffield*, replaced Type 42s lost in the Falklands War), and four Batch 3s.

F 88

Pauk Class

Origin:	USSR.
Displacement:	480 tons standard; 580 tons full load.
Dimensions:	Length overall 191.9ft (58.5, beam 2.15ft (9.8m); draught 8.2ft (2.5m).
Propulsion:	2 M517 diesels; 20,000shp;two shafts.
Performance:	32 knots; 2,000nm at 20 knots.
Built:	1977 onwards.
Ships:	22 in service; more building.
Complement:	40.
Armament:	1 76.2mm DP gun, 1 SA-N-5/8 SAM launcher (4 missiles plus 16 reloads), 1 30mm CIWS, 2 RBU ASW launchers, 4 single ASW torpedo launchers, 2 depth charge racks (12 charges).

The Soviet Navy has had considerable experience in protecting the very long coastline of the USSR. To fulfil this mission they have developed a series of small warships for close-in protection, ranging from 200 ton fast-attack craft, such as the Stenka class, to 1,000 ton corvettes, such as the Petya and Grisha classes. The latest type in the middle of this bracket is the Pauk class. "Pauk" is the Russian word for "spider" and has been allocated by NATO; the correct Soviet name is not known, although the type designation is known to be "maly protivolodochny korabl" (small anti-submarine ship = corvette).

An unknown number of the Pauk class ships are also operated by the maritime arm of the KGB Border Guard. These appear to be equipped and armed identically with the naval version.

Class History

The *Pauk* design is especially interesting as being one of the smallest specialised anti-submarine ships in any contemporary navy. It was first seen by Western observers in 1980 and the Pauk is intended to be the replacement for the ageing Poti class. The Pauk class is in full production at three yards: Yaroslavl, Khabarovsk and one other; 22 are in service and the type looks likely to remain in production for several years yet.

In an unusual step for the Soviet Navy, the hull is identical with that of the Tarantul class and is of a neat, workmanlike design. However, the Pauk's propulsion system is all-diesel, with an assessed 20,000shp giving a maximum speed in the region of 28 to 32 knots, whereas the Tarantul has a COGOG system, giving a maximum speed of 36 knots.

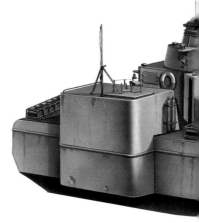

Right: With the Pauk, Soviet designers have yet again managed to cram large quantities of weapons and sensors into a compact hull to produce a well-balanced combat capability. The quad SA-N-5 launcher is obscured by the large sonar housing in this view, but the twin depth-charge racks and two of the four 16in (406mm) ASW torpedo tubes are visible. A single 3in (76.2mm) automatic gun and two RBU-1200 ASW rocket launchers are forward of the bridge, with a 30mm CIWS system aft.

Armament

The Soviet Navy's predeliction for packing the maximum firepower on to any given size of hull is again borne out in the Pauk class. The heaviest weapon is a single 3in (76.2mm) gun in a dual-purpose mounting on the forecastle. With a range of 15,310 yards (14,000m) against surface targets and an effective slant range against airborne targets of 22,966ft (7,000m) it has a rate of fire of 120rpm. It is controlled by a Bass Tilt radar director.

Main air defence system is an SA-N-5/8 (Grail/Gremlin) missile system. SA-N-5 is the naval version of the Soviet Army's shoulder-launched SA-7, whilst SA-N-8 is the naval version of the newer SA-14. Both missiles use visual aiming and IR homing and both use the same 4-missile manned launcher or single shoulder-launching tube. In the Pauk the missile launcher is mounted on the quarterdeck.

For close-in air defence against aircraft and missiles there is an ADMG-630 six-barrelled Gatling CIWS mounted high on the after superstructure. With a rate of fire of some 3,000 rounds per minute this is controlled either by the same Bass Tilt as the 76.2mm DP or by a remote optical director.

Principle ASW weapons systems are four, midships-mounted, single UTR ASW torpedo tubes, firing 16in (406mm) electric- powered, acoustic-homing torpedoes. There are also two five- barrelled RBU-1200 ASW rocket launchers mounted just forward of the bridge and two racks at the stern, each carrying six depth-charges.

Below: The RBU launcher system on the Pauk fires either 250mm or 300mm ASW rockets at ranges of up to 1,300yds (1200m).

There is a curious side-deck on the starboard side abreast the mast, which serves no readily apparent purpose apart from giving roof cover for one of the four torpedo tubes; it may be for a future weapons or sensor system. Various modifications have been incorporated during the production run, including additional sonar and raising the pilot-house by one half-deck.

The Tarantul's weapons system differs from the Pauk's in that two twin SS-N-2C SSM launchers are mounted each side of the superstructure, replacing the latter's torpedo tubes, and a second ADMG-630 is located aft. The *Tarantul* does not, of course, have any dipping sonars.

Sensors

As with other Soviet warships, the *Pauk* class corvettes seem covered in antennas, giving a good indication of the sensor fit. There is a Spin Trough navigation radar, an air/surface search system. There is also a Bass Tilt scanner, mounted prominently between the bridge and mast, which controls the fire of both 76.2mm and 30mm guns. There is also a back-up optical director for the 30mm Gatling system.

There is a hull-mounted MF sonar and also a dipping sonar housed in a box 10.5ft (3.2m) long, 10.5ft (3.2m) wide and 13.8ft (4.2m) high inset into the transom with a 4.26ft (1.3m) overhang. One of the more recent modifications is the addition of a second dipping sonar (apparently the same type as used by Helix ASW helicopters), which is housed in a special cabinet on the starboard quarter.

IFF systems include two Square Head and one High Pole. There are also passive EW arrays and two chaff launchers.

Conclusion

It seems probable that the Pauk, having conclusively proved itself in service, will continue in production for some years to come. As with so many other classes, the Soviet naval architects have managed to pack a great deal into a small hull and this class represents a substantial addition to the Soviet short-range ASW forces. Western ship designers would do well to take note of this class, which will undoubtedly be built in large numbers.

Left: Large numbers of small combatants such as the Pauk are in service with both the Soviet Navy and the KGB maritime border guard. The Pauk has probably the most effective anti-submarine capability of any vessel of this size.

Below: This Pauk seen in the Baltic shows the extensive electronics and sensor fit carried by the class. Later Pauk variants have been seen with the main pilothouse raised a half-deck higher than that shown on this earlier example.

Typhoon Class (All specifications are approximate.)

Origin:	USSR.
Displacement:	Surfaced 18,500 tons; submerged 25,000 tons.
Dimensions:	Length overall 561ft (171m); beam 78.74ft (24m); draught 41ft (12.5m).
Propulsion:	Nuclear — 2 330-360MW pressurised water reactors; 2 shafts.
Performance:	25 knots (submerged).
Built:	1975 to 1995.
Boats:	Built, 5; building, 3.
Complement:	150.
Armament:	Torpedo tubes — 6 21in (533mm) or 25.6in (650mm). Missiles — 20 SS-N-20 SLBM 21in (533mm) torpedoes or SS-N-15/16 ASW missiles.

The Soviet Navy was the first to develop ballistic-missile armed submarines — the Zulu IV class of 1955 armed with two SS-N-4 mounted vertically in the fin. From that start the SSBN, as it is known today, developed, with 12 or 16 SLBMs mounted vertically in a whaleback behind the sail. Thus, the Soviet Yankee and Delta classes were matched by the American Washington and Lafayette, British Resolution and French Le Redoutable classes. In the 1980s however, both the United States and the USSR have broken away from this pattern. First to appear was the US Navy's Ohio class, which, at 18,700 tons (submerged), was more than twice the size of any previous SSBN. More significant was the fact that it mounted no less than 24 missiles, an increase of 50 per cent. Then, as so often in recent years, the Soviet Navy took the West by surprise, producing a totally new type of SSBN — the Typhoon class — which was not only far larger than even the Ohio class, but also mounted 20 missiles in front of the sail.

Class History
Persistent rumours in Western naval circles about a new giant submarine were confirmed in November 1980 by the NATO announcement that the USSR had launched the first of the Typhoon class SSBNs. This event created great interest, not only because this was the first totally new Soviet SSBN design for 20 years, but also because of the sheer size of this enormous craft. Its submerged displacement of 25,000 tons, and overall length of 561ft (171m) made it by far the largest submarine ever built.

Among many unusual features of the design is the 78.74ft (24m) beam; the normal length:beam ratio in SSBNs is in the region of 13:1, but the extraordinary girth of the Typhoon reduces this to 7:1. At first this was thought to indicate a considerable degree of separation between concentric outer and inner hulls, or simply a huge inner hull. It is now agreed, however, that the most

Above: Pictures such as this do not really convey the size of the Typhoon SSBNs. With a length of 561ft (171m) and displacement of 25,000 tons, they are the largest submarines ever built, by a very wide margin.

Top: A Typhoon class SSBN at sea. The cylindrical pressure-hull at the foot of the sail is believed to house the combat control centre. The triangular structures on the after casing probably house TV cameras, while the square hatches immediately in front of them house communications buoys.

probable explanation is that the single outer hull encloses two separate side-by-side pressure hulls, containing the propulsion and missile units, with a third pressure hull above them at the foot of the sail containing the control centre and a fourth pressure hull forward containing the torpedo tubes.

If boats of the Typhoon class were to venture out into the open oceans, it would seem to be relatively easy for opposing ASW forces to detect them — their very size facilitates detection by many means. Conversely, the large volume of the hull makes quietening, a major problem in SSBN design, rather easier. One possibility would seem to be that the Typhoon class is simply intended to be a relatively invulnerable missile launching platform. A boat would be required only to move out a short distance across the Barents Sea to the Arctic ice-cap and to loiter there, its time on station limited only by the endurance of the crew. It would launch its missiles by rising to the surface, breaking through the ice and then firing while on the surface. For the latter role conditions can be assumed to be more spacious and comfortable than in any previous SSBN. There is, however, one other possibility: that the *Typhoon* is designed to operate for protracted periods a long way from its bases. The 4,300nm (7,240 km) range of its SS-N-20 SLBMs would certainly make it feasible for it to operate in the southern oceans, thus posing a threat to the United States from completely new directions.

Armament
The principal armament of the Typhoon is its 20 SS-N-20 SLBMs located in launching canisters forward of the sail in two rows of ten; the SS-N-20 has 6 to 9 MIRVed warheads and a range of 4,300nm (7,240km). A battery of torpedo tubes is located forward of the missile compartment, and, apart from conventional torpedoes, these may well be used for cruise missiles (e.g. SS-N-21) and minelaying; both weapons would be very useful if the Typhoon's role is in distant waters. One advantage of its unique layout is that all weapons

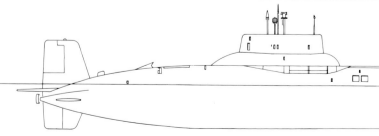

are concentrated in one integrated area forward of the combat control centre.

In a test observed by American satellites in October 1982 the first Typhoon launched two missiles within 15 seconds. This is a significant development as in all other known cases SSBNs have to fire their missiles at intervals of about 40 to 60 seconds.

Sensors

Little is published in the West about Soviet submarine sensors. However, it can safely be assumed that the Typhoon class is equipped with an active/passive sonar transducer, located in the bows, with conformal arrays along the hull for detection and fire control. There are large hatches on the after casing for VLF buoys.

The huge sail contains an extensive array of masts. First, there are the search and attack periscopes carried by all submarines. Most prominent in photographs is the large cylindrical array mounted atop a very sturdy mast; this is a combination of Snoop Pair and Rim Hat for surface surveillance and ESM. There is also Park Lamp for VLF/LF reception, Pert Spring for satellite navigation and Shot Gun for VHF communications. There is also a number of electro-optical sensors, whose purpose is not yet clear.

Conclusion

The sheer size of the Typhoon class boats causes much comment in the West. However, it is worth noting that the Soviets have frequently exhibited a fascination with size and have built extremely large aircraft and ships for many years. Their latest ship classes of battlecruiser *(Kirov)*, aircraft carrier *(Kiev)*, SSGN *(Oscar)* and the *Typhoon* — all seem to fit in with this general pattern. American sources suggest that the Soviets intend to build a total of eight Typhoons.

Left: A US official artist's drawing of the Typhoon, produced before photographs became available, but which has proved to be very accurate. It is believed that the huge outer casing houses two long pressure-hulls, each containing ten missiles and a nuclear powerplant, with a third smaller pressure-hull beneath the sail, housing the combat control centre. The twin propellers are unusual in modern submarines but are necessary in view of the Typhoons' huge size. Typhoons deploy from specially constructed bases in the Kamchatka Peninsula to patrol areas under the Arctic ice.

Left: Side elevation of the Typhoon. Every other SSBN design has the sail forward of the missile compartment, but the Typhoon is unique in reversing this, its 20 SS-N-20 missiles being located in two rows of ten forward of the sail. The full reason for this is not yet known to Western naval experts.

Los Angeles Class

Origin: United States.
Displacement: Surfaced 6,080 tons; submerged 6,900 tons.
Dimensions: Length overall 360ft (109.7m); beam 33ft (10.1m); draught 32.3ft (9.9m).
Propulsion: 1 pressurised water-cooled S6G nuclear reactor; 2 geared turbines; 35,000shp; 1 shaft.
Performance: 30 knots (submerged); maximum diving depth 1,476ft (450m).
Built: 1972 onwards to mid-1990s.
Boats: Built 45; building 14, ordered, 7.
Complement: 12 officers; 115 to 127 ratings.
Armament: Torpedo tubes: 4 21in (533mm) for firing conventional torpedoes, Subroc and Mark 48 ASW torpedoes; tube-launched Tomahawk SLCM in boats SSN 688 to SSN720. Vertical launch tubes: 15 for Tomahawk SLCM from SSN 721 onwards.

With the advent of nuclear propulsion, attack submarines have been freed from the periodic need to return to the surface to replenish their air supplies and to recharge batteries. This has made possible today's SSNs, which are highly-sophisticated vessels capable of operating for protracted periods at great depths and of travelling at great speeds, although such speeds may not be compatible with remaining silent and undetected.

Below: Over 66 Los Angeles class SSNs are to be launched.

One role for SSNs is to act in concert with SSBNs to ensure that they are undetected and unmolested by hostile submarines. The second is to search for hostile SSBNs themselves. The third is to act as part of the screen for a task group. The five navies currently operating SSNs, are the United States Navy (94), Soviet Navy (79), Royal Navy (15), French Navy (4) and People's Republic of China Navy (4).

Above: A Los Angeles class SSN running on the surface. These submarines represent one of the most successful programmes ever undertaken — 66 boats built over a period of some 20 years.

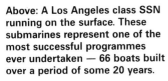

Left: All Los Angeles class SSNs are armed with four torpedo tubes located amidships to free the bow for the large sonar array. These can launch torpedoes, with 22 reloads. In earlier boats these tubes are also used to launch Tomahawk missiles, but in SSN-719 onwards the Tomahawks are housed in vertical launch tubes mounted in the bows, thus enabling the full load of torpedoes to be carried once again.

Class History

Both by far the largest and the most numerous SSNs are the boats of the Los Angeles class operated by the United States Navy. One of the most sophisticated, expensive, effective and important weapons systems in service today, the class is currently 45-strong, and will build up to an eventual class total of 66 in the mid-1990s. The origins of the class go back to the 1960s when the US Navy considered two classes of future SSNs: one was to be a high-speed attack and ASW submarine, and the second a very quiet type intended for "barrier" operations.

The latter requirement led to the USS *Glenard P Lipscomb* (SSN 685), launched in 1973. It had many interesting features aimed at achieving silent running. The most important of these was her propulsion unit, a Westinghouse S5WA natural-circulation reactor driving a turbo-electric plant, a system which removes the requirement for gearing, one of the prime sources of noise in nuclear submarines.

The first element of the 1960s programme, the high-speed ASW type, became the *Los Angeles* (SSN 688). The US Navy decided that, rather than go in for the considerable extra expense of two separate classes, the *Los Angeles* could perform both roles and the class was put into production. Although *Lipscomb* remains in front-line service, the turbo-electric drive system was not repeated in the Los Angeles class.

The Los Angeles boats are much larger than any previous American SSN being 57.8ft (17.63m) longer than the Sturgeon class, and the hull is optimised for high submerged speed, with a very small sail. One unfortunate outcome is that, because the sail-mounted planes cannot be rotated to the vertical, the boats of the Los Angeles class cannot break through ice. This problem will be overcome from USS *San Juan* (SSN 751) onwards. This boat will have its hydroplanes moved forward to the more traditional bow position and, together with some new electronic equipment, this will enable it to be declared "Arctic-capable".

There are plans to improve the Los Angeles boats, especially their sensors, weapons systems and control equipment. Such improvements will include moving the torpedo tubes back to the bow, and increasing their number to eight. Further, at least some of the Los Angeles boats will also probably get anechoic coatings, the first to be given to an American submarine.

Below: The Los Angeles class SSNs displace 6,900 tons submerged and have a speed in excess of 30 knots. Published diving depth is 1,476ft (450m).

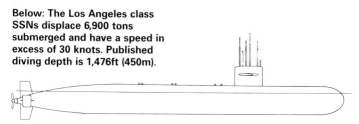

Armament

The most remarkable feature of the Los Angeles class is, however, its armament. These powerful submarines are armed with Subroc and Sub-Harpoon, as well as conventional and wire-guided torpedoes. All boats from SSN 688 to SSN 718 carry up to eight Tomahawk as part of their torpedo loads. All these are fired from the four 21in (533mm) torpedo tubes located amidships and angled outwards. From SSN 721 onwards, however, 15 vertical launch tubes for Tomahawk are being fitted in the space in the bow between the inner and outer hulls, thus restoring the torpedo capacity. So, although their primary mission is still to hunt other submarines and to protect SSBNs, the Los Angeles class boats can also be used without modification to sink surface ships at long-range with Sub-Harpoon, while Tomahawk enables them to operate against strategic targets well inland, as well. It has also been announced that from Fiscal Year 1985 the Los Angeles class will be given a mine-laying capability.

Above: USS *Salt Lake City* (SSN 716) on trials. The long fairing running down her starboard side houses the BQR-15 towed array.

Sensors

The sensor fit is comprehensive and includes the BQQ-5 sonar system in the bows and a passive tactical towed sonar array. The cable and winch are mounted in the ballast tanks, but there is no room for the array itself, which is, therefore, housed in a prominent fairing which runs along almost the entire length of the hull.

Conclusion

The Reagan Administration ordered a speeding-up of the Los Angeles building programme; three were completed in 1986, two in 1987 and three in 1988 and the rate is now stabilising at three per year. The Tomahawk missile programme was also accelerated, with these missiles being fitted in USS *Providence* (SSN 719) onwards. USS *Groton* (SSN 694) travelled around the world submerged between April 4 and October 8, 1980.

There has been much criticism of the complexity and cost of the Los Angeles class and it is alleged that too many sacrifices were made to achieve the very high speed. A design for a cheaper and smaller SSN, under consideration in 1980 as a result of Congressional pressure, was later shelved, but may well reappear, especially if the proposed new class should turn out to be even more expensive than the Los Angeles, which is certainly a possibility.

The Los Angeles class is very sophisticated and each boat is an extremely potent fighting machine. With a production run of at least 66 it must be considered an outstandingly successful design. However, these boats are becoming very expensive: the first cost $221.25 million, while the boat bought in 1979 cost $325.6 million, and the two in 1981 $495.8 million each.

Design work has already started on the next major class of SSNs for the US Navy — the Seawolf ("SSN 21") class. Among the major objectives in this very important programme are even better sound quieting and a greater under-ice capability than the Los Angeles class, both being intended to challenge the Soviet SSBNs and SSNs operating under the Arctic ice-cap. A noteworthy development is that the forward hydroplanes will be mounted on the bow rather than on the sail. It is also planned that the Seawolf class will carry many more weapons than today's SSNs. Under present plans the Seawolf boats will have eight torpedo tubes, with no less than 50 missiles, a mix of Sea Lance, Tomahawk, Sub-Harpoon, Mark 48 ADCAP torpedoes and mines.

A much more sophisticated and rapidly reacting command system is to be fitted, which will be operated by a crew of 8 officers and 118 ratings. Submerged displacement will be some 9,150 tons and the Seawolf boats will have a maximum underwater speed of some 35 knots, and a speed of up to 20 knots while remaining effectively silent. At least 28 boats are planned, with the first of class expected to join the fleet in 1994.

Upholder Class

Origin:	United Kingdom.
Displacement:	Submerged 2,400 tons; surfaced 2,185 tons.
Dimensions:	Length overall 230.5ft (70.26m); beam 24.9ft (7.6m); draught 18.0ft (5.5m).
Propulsion:	2 Paxman-Valenta, 16 RPA 200SZ 16-cylinder diesel generators,2,035hp each; 2 GEC 2,500kw alternators; 1 shaft.
Performance:	Maximum speed (submerged) 20 knots, (surfaced) 12 knots; range 10,000nm plus; endurance 49 days; typical patrol of 8 knots transit, 28 days in area at a radius of 2,100nm; maximum diving depth 820+ft (250+m).
Built:	1986 to 1992.
Boats:	*Upholder, Unseen; Ursula* (building), *Unicorn* (building).
Complement:	7 officers; 37 ratings.
Armament:	Torpedo tubes — 6 21in (533mm). with 18 Mark 24 or Spearfish torpedoes, or Sub-Harpoon SSM.

The diesel-electric submarine's history stretches in an unbroken line back to the submersibles built by John Holland in the United States at the end of the last century. A steadily increasing number of navies have started their own submarine arms, but it was not until the 1950s that the appearance of nuclear-powered submarines gave some choice in the means of propulsion. Of the five major navies, only the United States and the French have decided to adopt nuclear-propulsion exclusively. The other three (the USSR, Britain and the People's Republic of China), are continuing to produce both diesel-electric and nuclear-powered types, whilst all the remaining smaller navies remain committed exclusively to the diesel-electric submarine.

A number of diesel-electric classes are being produced with displacements in the region of 1,000 to 1,500 tons. However, there are also some large designs in production, such as the Japanese *Yuushio* (2,200 tons), the Dutch *Zeeleeuw* (2,800 tons) and the Soviet *Kilo* (3,000 tons). Of these, perhaps the most sophisticated type currently in production is the British *Upholder* class (2,400 tons), which incorporates many lessons learned from the development of four classes of SSN as well as a long historty of SSK production and operation.

Class History

The Upholder is based on the Vickers Type 2400 design, a private venture offered to several overseas navies. The single-hull form is based closely upon

Above: The Upholder class is probably the most sophisticated diesel-electric type in service.

that of the British SSNs and has a high beam-to-length ratio of 1:9.25, compared to 1:11 for the previous Oberon class. The pressure-hull is constructed of NQ-1 steel (equivalent to HY-80) and is sub-divided internally by two main bulkheads, with the two forward watertight compartments having two deck levels and the after (machinery) space a single deck. The outer hull is coated in elastomeric tiles, which muffle self-noise and reduce sonar returns, thus contributing to the exceptional "quietness" of the design. As with the *Oberons,* the skin of the sail is constructed of glass-reinforced plastic (GRP) to conserve weight.

The Upholder class has large battery capacity which gives a high underwater speed and endurance. Even so, there are plans that the fifth and subsequent boats will be stretched to accommodate even more batteries and more powerful motors, raising the surfaced displacement from 2,185 tons to 3,000 tons. As with all current non-nuclear submarines, the Upholders still need to snorkel, which can be done at speeds of up to 19 knots.

These boats are intended to be very reliable, being designed to operate for 15,000 hours (equivalent to 7 years in commission) between major refits. As with other modern SSK designs, a noteworthy economy in manpower is achieved by the greatly increased use of automation. This means that the Upholder class requires a crew of 7 officers and 37 ratings compared with 6 officers and 62 ratings for the Oberon class; a very significant and worthwhile 35 per cent reduction in scarce and expensive-to-train manpower.

Above: HMS *Upholder*, first of her class, is wheeled out of the VSEL building hall at Barrow-in-Furness, England. The platform on top of the bow is for spectators during the launch ceremony, but the covers lower down are intended to conceal the highly classified sonar installation. The entire hull is covered in anechoic tiles.

Armament
There are six bow-mounted 21in (533mm) torpedo tubes in two banks; two in the upper bank and four below. A further 12 reloads are carried for a total of 18, which can be a mix of Tigerfish torpedoes, Sub-Harpoon ASMs or Stonefish mines, and, in the future, Spearfish torpedoes.

Sensors
The principal sonar is the Type 2040, a development of the French Thompson-CSF-Argonaute passive system, whose cylindrical array takes up most of the bow, with intercept hydrophones arranged along the sides. There is also a Type 2046 "clip-on" towed array and a Type 20-19 PARIS (Passive/Active Range and Intercept Sonar).

There are six masts. As with all submarines, there are two periscopes. The search periscope is a Barr & Stroud CK 35, with a Decca EW array, while the

Below: This view shows the torpedo tubes and sonar in the bow, with the engine rooms at the rear. The centre of the hull is divided into two levels, with the command centre and torpedo storage above the accomodation areas.

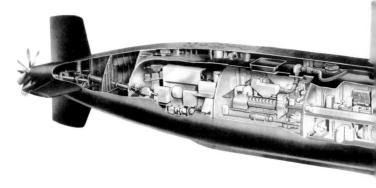

attack periscope is a Barr & Stroud CH85, with an infra-red capability. There are also, a mast for the Type 1007 surface radar and another for the communications antenna. Finally, there are the snort induction and exhaust masts.

Conclusion

Currently four Upholder class are on order: HMS *Upholder* was commissioned in 1988 and the remaining three units will join the fleet in 1991, 1992 and 1993, respectively. However, it is believed that the Royal Navy's eventual target is ten boats, with the fifth onwards being of a stretched design with a displacement of 3,000 tons (surfaced), capable of greater endurance. As several types of air-independent propulsion systems are now under development and, in some cases, actually on trial, it may be assumed that the British Upholder class may be the among the last of the diesel-electric type, which have served navies so well for so many years.

Above: The launch of HMS *Upholder*, 2 December 1986, the first British diesel-electric submarine to be launched since HMS *Onyx* on 18 August 1966. Four have been ordered so far, but the eventual intention is for a class of twelve.

Wasp Class

Origin:	United States.
Displacement:	28,233 tons light; 40,532 tons full load.
Dimensions:	Length overall 844.2ft (257.3m); beam 140ft (42.67m); draught 26.7ft (8.13m).
Propulsion:	2 sets of gas turbines; 77,000shp; 2 shafts.
Performance:	24 knots; 9,500nm at 20 knots.
Built:	1985 onwards for mid-1990s.
Boats:	*Wasp* (LHD 1), *Essex* (LHD 2), *Kearsarge* (LHD 3), (unnamed) (LHD 4).
Complement:	Ship's crew 98 officers, 982 ratings, plus 1,873 embarked troops.
Armament:	2 Mk 29 SAM launchers (each with 8 Sea Sparrow or 6 Sea Sparrow and 10 RAM), 3 Phalanx CIWS, 8 12.7mm AAM mg.
Aircraft:	(Assault role) — 30-32 CH-46 helicopters (or less CH-53), 6 AV-8B Harriers. (ASW/Carrier role) — 20 AV-8B Harrier, 4-6 SH-60B helicopters.

The US Navy has for many years possessed the largest amphibious warfare fleet in the world. This is a result, in part, of participating in the D-day landings in Europe in 1944, but more importantly of the Pacific Campaign from 1942 to 1945. The shipping developed for the latter campaign stood the US Navy in good stead well into the post-war era, but eventually needed to be first supplemented and later replaced by new-build ships.

World War II saw the start of three strands in the development of amphibious warfare shipping. First, at the lower end, were Tank Landing Craft (LCT), vessels of some 3,000 to 4,000 tons full load displacement with a clear vehicle deck and a flat, ramped bow.

Second were Tank Landing Ships (LST). They are somewhat larger than LCTs and have a ship bow. The US Navy's Newport class were built in the 1960s. With a 8,450 tons full load displacement they can carry 500 tons of cargo and up to 431 troops.

This view shows USS Wasp on sea trials before delivery, with no helicopters or aircraft embarked. (Ingalls Shipbuilding photo).

The third, and larger, type is the Landing-Ship Dock (LSD) in which a large internal dock is used to transport and load small landing craft. Such ships almost invariably also operate helicopters from a flight deck above the dock.

These three strands in development have produced the modern concept of the large amphibious assault ship. It cannot land troops and vehicles direct onto a beach, but depends instead upon helicopters operating from a large flight-deck. Early in this field was the US Navy's Iwo Jima class, seven ships of 18,300 tons full load displacement, and capable of carrying 1,900 troops.

Follow-on to the Iwo Jima class is the Tarawa class multi-purpose assault transport (LHA), very much larger (39,400 tons full load displacement) and with greatly increased capability. These impressive ships have the general appearance of an aircraft-carrier, with a full-length flight-deck, superstructure offset to starboard and elevators. They also have an 262.5ft (80m) x 76.8ft (23.4m) dock for LCU 1610 class landing ships.

Class History

The Wasp class is to be the successor to the Tarawa class. It is slightly larger, but with the important additional capability of being able to operate as an ASW carrier, as well as an assault transport. The flight-deck is constructed of HY-100 steel and is designed to operate both helicopters and AV-8B Harriers. Consideration was given to installing a "ski-jump" take-off ramp for the Harriers, but this was eventually not pursued as it was considered more important to maximise the number of helicopter deck landing spots. The stern elevator, on the port-side in the Tarawa class, has been moved to the starboard in the Wasp.

These ships can carry up to 1,873 troops (2,073 in austere conditions) and have 22,896ft² (2,127m²) of vehicle parking space and 109,000ft³ (3,087m³) dry cargo storage. Troops and vehicles are moved ashore by helicopter or landing craft. Some 30 to 32 CH-46 transport helicopters, or a smaller number of CH-53s, can be carried, together with six AV-8B Harriers. The dock is shorter and narrower than on the Tarawas, taking three LCACs or 12 LCM(6) and has a horizontally-hinged stern-gate, again unlike the Tarawas, (which have a sectional, rising gate).

In the ASW role the Wasp class will carry 20 AV-8B Harriers and 4 to 6 SH-60B Seahawk LAMPS-III ASW helicopters. However, the ships carry no sonars or ASW weapons systems of their own.

The first ship, the *Wasp* (LHD 1) entered service in March 1989 and will be followed by the *Essex* (LHD 2) in 1992 and *Kearsarge* (LHD 3) in 1993. LHD 4 (as yet un-named) is scheduled to be ordered in Fiscal Year 1989 and LHD 5 in Fiscal Year 1991.

Armament

Armament is relatively light for a ship of this size. The primary weapons systems are two Mark 29 launchers for NATO Sea Sparrow or RAM air defense missiles. These are supplemented by three Vulcan/Phalanx CIWS and a multiple 12.7mm machine-gun mount.

Aircraft

In the amphibious role the Wasps will carry 30 to 32 CH-46 or a lesser number of GH-53 helicopters. Six US Marine Corps AV-8B Harriers will be embarked for ground attack missions in support of the marine forces ashore. In the ASW aircraft carrier role the Wasps will carry 20 AV-8Bs and between four and six SH-60B LAMPS-III Seahawk helicopters.

Conclusion

The Wasp class shows a new trend in warship design. Previous amphibious carriers such as the Tarawa class in the US Navy and, albeit to a possibly lesser extent, the Soviet Ivan Rogov, have been dedicated to their amphibious role. However, the Wasps deliberately incorporate the ability to undertake both the amphibious warfare and ASW roles. Such a dual capability is, however, obtained only through a very large ship and at considerable financial cost.

Sacramento Class

Origin: United States.
Displacement: 18,700 tons standard; 56,600 tons full load.
Dimensions: Length overall 792.0ft (241.4m); beam 107.9ft (32.9m); draught 38ft (11.6m).
Propulsion: 2 General Electric geared turbines; 100,000shp; 2 shafts.
Performance: 26 knots; 6,000nm at 26 knots,10,000nm at 17 knots.
Built: 1961 to 1969.
Ships: *Sacramento* (AOE 1), *Camden* (AOE 2), *Seattle* (AOE 3), *Detroit* (AOE 4).
Complement: 600 (33 officers, 567 ratings).
Armament: 1 Mark 29 Sea Sparrow SAM (6 missiles), 2 Phalanx CIWS, 4 12.7mm AA mg.
Aircraft: 2 UH-46 helicopters.

The concept of a sea-train keeping the warships of a fleet constantly topped up with fuel, ammunition, spare parts and provisions was brought to a high state of perfection by the US Navy in the Pacific campaign in World War II. Since then the systems have been steadily improved, although the only major innovation has been the use of helicopters for vertical replenishment (VERTREP).

Traditionally, most navies have operated four types of single-role combat support ships: fleet oilers (AO), ammunition ships (AE), stores ships (AF) and cargo ships (AK). However, there has been a move to produce ships which can perform more than one of these roles. For example, the Royal Navy currently has two main types of support ship: fleet replenishment ships, which carry ammunition, explosives, food and stores; and fleet oilers, which carry fuel oil, diesel, aircraft fuel and lubricating oil.

Class History
Currently the largest underway replenishment ships in any navy, the four American ships of the Sacramento class were designed to keep a carrier battle group supplied with all its needs. Further, they were designed to provide a "one-stop" service, with all types of dry and liquid replenishment available in one hull. They thus needed exceptionally high speed necessary for them to keep pace with carrier battle groups and a large carrying capacity.

The first of the class, *Sacramento* (AOE 1), was completed in 1963 and the *Detroit* (AOE 4), in 1969. A proposed fifth unit AOE 5, was cancelled when construction costs turned out to be higher than planned.

Below: The Sacramento class USS Seattle (right) refuels the combat stores ship USS San Diego (left) at sea.

Although quite different in role and time, the Sacramento class ships have an interesting relationship with the Iowa class battleships. *Sacramento* (AOE 1) and *Camden* (AOE 2) each have half the machinery intended for *Kentucky* (BB 66), while *Seattle* (AOE 3) and *Detroit* (AOE 4) have the machinery for *Illinois* (BB 65), both these battleships having been cancelled and broken up in the 1950s. This not only reduced the building costs of these expensive ships, but proved a further bonus when the Iowa class battleships were reactivated in the 1980s, since the engineering expertise necessary to operate the 600lb steam plant still existed among the engineers manning the AOEs.

Armament

All four ships of the Sacramento class were originally armed with four twin 3in (76mm) gun mounts. The forward two were removed in the 1970s and replaced by a single NATO Sea Sparrow launcher, while the second two were replaced by two Vulcan/Phalanx CIWS in the 1980s. There is also one quadruple 12.7mm machine-gun mounting.

Role equipment

Cargo capacity is 23,718 tons of oil, 2,150 tons of munitions and 750 tons of provisions. The Sacramento class was one of the first two designs to employ the fast automatic shuttle transfer (FAST) system, which revolutionised the handling of stores and munitions. In this system "M"-frames with automatic tensioning devices replaced the conventional king-posts and booms. There are four refuelling stations to port and two to starboard, and there are three contant-tension transfer stations for dry stores to port and four to starboard. There is a large helicopter deck aft with a three-bay hangar for VERTREP helicopters, although normal helicopter complement is two Boeing-Vertol UH-46 Sea Knights.

Camden (AOE 2) is currently being used to test the new "standard US Navy UNREP" suite. This includes new winches, rams, ram-tensioners and control booths.

Conclusion

The Sacramento class proved to be very expensive to construct, even with the "free" propulsion units from the cancelled battleships and a fifth ship (AOE 5) was cancelled. The next class to be built by the US Navy was the seven-ship Wichita class replenishment oilers (AOR). With a capacity to transport liquid fuels (23,450 tons), ammunition (600 tons) and provisions (575 tons) their engines can produce only 32,000shp (compared to the 100,000shp of the Sacramentos), resulting in a maximum speed of 20 knots, substantially less than that of the more expensive AOEs.

With four Sacramento and seven Wichita class replenishment ships the US Navy is four short of its requirement to provide logistic support for 15 carrier battle groups. Thus, a new class of AOEs is being built, with the lead ship, *Supply* (AOE 6) (48,800 tons) due to enter service in 1991, under the designation "multiproduct station ship". The design of these ships is based upon that of the Sacramento class, but is obviously updated and upgraded, with improved stores handling and better protective systems. Overall capacity is slightly less: liquid fuels (21,000 tons); munitions (1,800 tons), refrigerated stores (400 tons) and other dry stores (150 tons). Power is provided by four General Electric LM-2500 gas turbines, to give the same 100,000shp as in the Sacramento class, with a similar speed of 26 knots. The US Navy currently plants to build four of this effective class.

The only foreign vessel remotely comparable to the Sacramento and Supply classes is the Soviet Navy's *Berezhina*, which was built in the mid-1970s and remains the sole ship of its class in the Soviet fleet. With a 36,000 ton full load displacement and a maximum speed of 22 knots, *Berezhina*'s capacity is estimated to be: fuel oil, 16,000 tons; fresh water, 500 tons; and dry stores 2,000 to 3,000 tons. However, with only two abeam and one astern refuelling stations, two solid stores transfer rigs and VERTREP facilities its capabilities are not as great as those of the American AOE ships.

Fleet Support for Modern Naval Forces

The support of warships at sea is one of the lesser-known and possibly less glamorous tasks in a modern navy, and yet it is absolutely crucial to success in combat. All warships contain a finite amount of consumables and their consumption of some items is very heavy. Further, in order to maintain the greatest degree of combat flexibility warship captains endeavour to keep "topped-up" as much as possible so that, if an unseen situation arises, they have the maximum possible endurance, without having to return to port before proceeding to an operational area. In 1982, for example, at the beginning of the Falklands War, the Royal Navy had to divert many warships direct from overseas tasks to the operational zone in the South Atlantic, which was some 8,000nm from their home base, with only the very limited facilities of remote Ascension Island available as a forward base. During that campaign one ship, the aircraft carrier HMS *Invincible* remained at sea for 166 days at a single stretch, a feat only made possible by efficient and effective Replenishment at Sea (RAS).

RAS has been practiced for many years. In the days of coal-firing it involved colliers coming alongside the warship and the manual transfer of huge volumes of coal — all in sacks. This could not be conducted while underway and was ideally done in sheltered water; it involved an intricate network of coaling stations and colliers waiting, sometimes for months at a time, at remote rendezvous points. The conversion to oil-fired propulsion made underway RAS feasible, but early efforts concentrated on the astern method, which proved to be slower, less flexible and less efficient than the abeam method. This latter method was pioneered by the US Navy in World War II and brought to a high degree of perfection in the Pacific Campaign 1942-45.

In naval terms RAS means the restocking of ships with fuel, ammunition and missiles for both ships and embarked aircraft, together with provisions, stores, aircraft spares, water and men. Ship-to-ship replenishment may, of course, be done in sheltered water with both ships stationary as, for example, between a depot ship and a submarine or destroyer lying alongside. However, much more common is underway replenishment, which can either be between specially equipped ships and warships, or between larger and smaller warships.

In World War II most "blue-water" navies operated three types of replenishment ship, supplying fuel oil and lubricants, munitions and dry stores, respectively. In the 1960s munitions and stores ships tended to combine, leaving two types in use, but today there is a further move towards a "one-stop" replenishment vessel. As we have seen, this started with the US Navy's Sacramento class, large and very fast ships, designated "Fast Combat Support Ships" (AOE) and powered by the engines intended for the two cancelled Iowa class battleships. Designed specifically to keep pace with Carrier Battle Groups (CVBG), these four ships are still in service, but proved so expensive to construct (despite the "free" engines) and run that there was some reluctance to repeat them and the succeeding Wichita class of "Replenishment Oilers" (AOR) was slower and cheaper. In the early-1980s, however, it was decided to develop a new AOE, the Supply class, which are updated versions of the Sacramento design.

The US Navy's AOEs need their high speed to operate in company with a CVBG. The British Fort Victoria class AORs, now building, are designed to operate with Royal Navy ASW groups, thus requiring less speed, which can be achieved without undue expense. In the case of the USSR it is noteworthy that although their most modern AOR, *Berezhina*, seems a capable design, surprisingly no sister ship has been built since she was completed in 1978.

Below: RFA *Olmeda* (A 124) replenishes HMS *Invincible* at sea. Such complicated looking evolutions are, in fact, absolutely routine and are essential to keep warships at sea for protracted periods.

Transfer of Solid Stores

Typical of methods of transfer of solid stores are the three types of rig used for abeam transfer in the Royal Navy: light jackstay, heavy jackstay and GEC Mark II RAS system. The light jackstay is used for transferring light stores in single loads up to an absolute maximum of 496lb (225kg), or men or stretchers. The rig consists of a jackstay between the two ships, with a traveller block moving along it, from which is slung the load. The traveller and load are hauled between the two ships by an outhaul in the receiving ship and an inhaul in the delivering ship, manned by groups of sailors in each ship.

The heavy jackstay is basically a much stronger version, capable of taking loads up to 20 tonnes. In this case the jackstay is a steel wire controlled by an automatic-tensioning winch on the delivering ship, while the outhaul and inhaul, which control the traveller's progress, are worked by winches. Stores and ammunition are transferred using slings, cargo nets or special containers.

The current primary method uses the GEC Mark II RAS system, which requires both ships to be fitted with special arms and involves a continuous, constant-tension jackstay. The delivering ship is fitted with a frame in which the hydraulically-operated supply arm can move vertically to raise the load. The receiving ship is fitted with a hydraulically-operated receiving arm, with the loop of the jackstay being taken to a pair of winch drums. These control the tensioning of the rig and the rate of movement of the traveller between both ships

VERTREP (VERtical REPlenishment) is undertaken by helicopters, normally using underslung loads carried in cargo nets or pallets, suspended from a cargo release unit beneath the aircraft. A typical cargo net has a safe working load of 3,000lb (1,360kg). Pallets can normally take loads of 1 or 2 tonnes, but the limiting factor is usually the sling, which typically has a limit of 2,240lb (1,016kg).

Below: Solid stores are transferred on a jackstay. The load is slung from a traveller block, which is being pulled across by the outhaul (on the ship to the left of the picture), while the inhaul on the delivering ship is allowed to run free. Behind the solid stores the transfer of fuel is taking place through two hoses.

Liquid Replenishment

The most common method of liquid refuelling is the "latched derrick probe rig", which is similar to the heavy jackstay rig described above for transferring solids, except that the jackstay is used to support three travellers from which the fuel hose is suspended. The ships travel at the set distance apart and, as with all RAS systems, initial contact is established using a gun-line, which is used to pass across the 1in (28mm) steel-wire jackstay. Once this is secured and tensioned the hose is hauled across on its three travellers, each of which is connected to the delivering ship by a wire for recovery at the end of the operation. The hose then hangs in three large loops, but the final 15ft (4.5m) length is suspended close to the jackstay by three trolleys and terminates in a probe which mates with a receiver on the receiving ship. The receiver is bell-mouthed, angled at 90 degrees and supported by a swivel arm it to compensate for movements of the probe.

Above: USS *Saratoga* (CV 60) dwarfs the 35,000 ton Mispillion class USNS *Navasota* (T AO 106), a fleet oiler of Military sealift Command.

Below: The scene on board RFA *Regent* (A-486), a British replenishment ship, as she herself receives fuel from RFA *Olmeda*.

VERTREP

In the 1960s replenishment ships began to be fitted with flight-decks for VERTREP using helicopters from the receiving ships. Then hangars were added so that the replenishment ships could carry their own VERTREP helicopters. More recently many navies have decided that it would be wasteful not to exploit the full capabilities of all available flight-decks and helicopters and now many replenishment ships carry helicopters capable of ASW and anti-ship missions, as well as, of course, VERTREP. The new British Fort Victoria class AORs will carry three EH-101 helicopters and the US Navy's Supply class will also be able to accommodate three similar large resupply helicopters.

The current standard US Navy VERTREP aircraft is the Boeing Vertol UH-46D Sea Knight, a twin-rotor helicopter which can carry up to 3,000lb (1360kg) internally or 10,000lb (4,536kg) underslung. The Sikorsky CH-53E Super Stallion is also used in the VERTREP role, if available, although none are actually stationed aboard replenishment ships. CH-53s can carry up to 36,000lb (16,330kg)

underslung, a quantum increase in performance over the UH-46, although being very much larger they do have some problems delivering to smaller destroyers and frigates. One US Navy CH-53 squadron in the Mediterranean moved 2,232 tons of priority stores in one year in support of the Mediterranean Fleet. In the next generation it is likely that the US Navy will use the Boeing-Bell MV-22A Osprey "tilt-engine" aircraft for VERTREP tasks, with an underslung payload of 10,000lb (4,536kg).

The Royal Navy uses Westland Wessex and Westland Sea King helicopters for VERTREP, which are usually ASW aircraft doing VERTREP as a secondary task. The Soviet Navy uses specially adapted Kamov Hormone helicopters for VERTREP.

Other Ships

In addition to specialised replenishment ships, many larger warships can be used to carry stores and fuel for transfer to other ships in the group. For example, each of the US Navy's Iowa class battleships is fitted with a large outrigger for streaming fuel lines to accompanying warships in the battle group.

Left: A Royal Navy Wessex carries an underslung load between two ships at sea. VERTREP allows the transfer of stores without the difficult and time-consuming manoeuvre of moving ships alongside each other. Helicopters are also useful for transporting key personnel, essential stores and equipment from the shore to ships at sea.

Right: A typical task group would have at least one or two replenishment vessels in formation. This picture shows a transit formation with four warships escorting two fleet oilers and an ammunition ship. If attack was thought likely, the warships would be spread around the formation to provide anti-submarine and air defence, and there would be much greater separation between ships. Many supply ships now have some self-defence capability.

RAS Tactics

In the inter-war years, as the possibility of war with Japan became more obvious, the US Navy gave increasing consideration to the logistical support of task groups in the vast area of the Pacific. This led to the development of both techniques and tactics which still form the basis of RAS in modern navies. In the World War II Pacific Campaign the US Navy kept replenishment ships apart from battle fleets in an Underway Replenishment Group (URG). This would normally comprise three types of replenishment ship (for oil, stores and ammunition respectively), together with a number of escorts and a flagship for the group commander. Each warship would have a designated "replenishment day" which would involve it in withdrawing from the task group to rendezvous with the URG.

In an entirely unrelated and unique development, the German Navy in World War II introduced the concept of replenishing submarines at sea, using purpose-built supply submarines: the Type XIV. These carried 432 tons of fuel oil, 45 tons of provisions and four torpedoes to re-supply other boats, and were used to replenish operational U-boats far out in the Atlantic. However, radio messages giving details of rendezvous points were intercepted by the Allies and all ten boats of the class were sunk. As far as is known, this idea has not been repeated; indeed, the introduction of nuclear propulsion makes it largely redundant.

Today, although URGs may be used on occasions, it is far more likely that replenishment ships will travel in company with task groups, both to ensure instant RAS when needed and for the protection of the otherwise very vulnerable auxiliaries. It also follows that, if replenishment ships are to travel in company with battle groups (BG) in this way, they should also play a role in the BG's defence. Thus, most navies are now arming such auxiliaries. Many have at least some air defence weapons (for example, 40mm Bofors) while some US Navy ships, such as the Wichita, Sacramento and Supply classes mount Mark 15 CIWS and NATO Sea Sparrow missile systems. British Royal Fleet Auxiliary (RFA) vessels have been very lightly armed for many years, but this has been changed since the Falklands War and the new Fort Victoria class AORs will have Sea Wolf air defence missile systems. In addition, as stated above, many modern auxiliaries use their flight-decks, initially installed for use in VERTREP, to operate ASW helicopters.

Ships undergoing RAS are naturally very vulnerable to hostile attack, particularly from aircraft or submarines. Ships therefore zig-zag, altering course by 5 or 10 degrees at a time, under control of the delivering ship. Further, to reduce the chances of electronic intercepts, the delicate operation is controlled by light or flag signals. There may also be non-hostile emergencies and all ships involved must, therefore, always be prepared for a sudden breakaway, which can be initiated by any ship. In all except the direst emergency every attempt is made to avoid actual destruction or loss of the gear, which would be difficult to replace at sea.

Other Support Ships

Modern fleets require many support and auxiliary ships. Such vessels are manned either by regular navy personnel or by civilian crews, provided by organisations such as the US Military Sealift Command (MSC) and the British RFA.

Immediate support for combat ships is provided by repair ships, which can provide second line repair.

During the Falklands War the Royal Navy made excellent use of MV *Stena Seaspread* (10,900 tons), a civilian oilfield support vessel chartered for the conflict, which carried out major repairs at sea, even in the inhospitable waters of the South Atlantic. As a result MV *Stena Inspector* was purchased and commissioned as RFA *Diligence*, and has since supported naval operations in the Falklands and the Persian Gulf. Other major navies

Below: The M.V. Atlantic Conveyor was used during the Falklands war to transport essential military supplies. These Harriers were flown off before the ship was sunk by an Argentine Exocet SSM.

also have repair ships, those of the US Navy and the Soviet Navy being much larger.

Major navies also use large auxiliary vessels as tenders for submarines and destroyers, primarily to provide floating base facilities for squadrons of such warships deployed overseas or in remote areas. For example, the US Navy has deployed submarine tenders for many years to support Polaris and Poseidon SSBNs in overseas locations such as Scotland's Holy Loch. The US Navy's Spear class tenders (23,493 tons), provide support for up to 12 submarines, with four alongside at once; three of the class are specifically intended to support Los Angeles class SSNs. Simon Lake class tenders are designed to support Trident-equipped SSBNs, while the Hunley class support those with Poseidon SLBMs. The Soviet Navy has similar vessels, including the Aleskandr Brykin class (17,000 tons) tenders, (which transport SS-N-20 SLBMs for Typhoon SSBNs), and Ugra (9,600 tons) and Don class submarine tenders.

Other auxiliary vessels include salvage vessels, ocean-going and harbour tugs, training ships, barracks ships, floating docks and the innumerable minor craft needed to support harbour facilities, trials, weapons development and reserve fleets, etc.

Three areas of considerable growth are those of oceanographic ships, intelligence collectors and ocean surveillance. Oceanographic ships are needed to map the ocean floor and to carry out research on the still largely unknown nature of the oceans themselves, primarily in support of submarines.

The Soviet Navy has operated a large fleet of "intelligence collectors" for many years, which make no attempt to disguise their electronic intelligence (ELINT) or signal intelligence (SIGINT) roles; indeed, they now carry Soviet "SSV" (Sudno Svyazyy) = Communications Vessel) pendant numbers.

Merchant Shipping

Even all these ships are insufficient for modern navies' needs in war and all have plans to expand their support shipping fleets in times of crisis. At its simplest this will involve chartering or impressing nationally-owned merchant ships. One navy to practice this is the Royal Navy, which refers to "Ships Taken Up From Trade" (STUFT). During the Falklands War, this practice was employed and a large number of British merchant ships, ranging from the liners Queen Elizabeth II and Canberra through North Sea ferries such as MV Norland to humble trawlers, took a very active part in the campaign. One such ship, the Atlantic Conveyor, was sunk.

The US Navy not only has similar plans for civilian ships, but also has the National Defense Reserve Fleet (NDRF). The key component of this is the Ready Reserve Force (RRF), which provides a back-up to the MSC fleet. These ships are held in large anchorages and are at 5-, 10- or 20-day readiness status, and are exercised regularly.

Below: Packed with electronic equipment, Soviet intelligence gatherers record and analyse NATO radar and communications signals to glean valuable operational and technical intelligence.

OTHER SUPER-VALUE MILITARY GUIDES IN THIS SERIES......

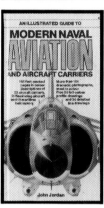